17.95

CURTAINS

CURTAINS

STEPHEN BILL

faber and faber
LONDON · BOSTON

First published in 1988
by Faber and Faber Limited
3 Queen Square London WC1N 3AU

Typeset by Goodfellow & Egan Ltd Cambridge
Printed in Great Britain by
Cox & Wyman Ltd Reading Berkshire

British Library Cataloguing in Publication Data

Bill, Stephen
Curtains.
I. Title
822′.914   PR6052.I772/

ISBN 0–571–15245–7

Contents

Introduction

Our only Instrument for Measuring Life is Death.
Jean Paul Marat

Although it is often a fruitless exercise to try working out where plays come from, I think in this instance I can pinpoint a seminal moment. It happened the last time I visited my grandmother in hospital. I entered the geriatric day-room, scanned the half-dead faces arranged neatly round the walls, arranged like in a waiting room – waiting for what? My grandmother appeared not to be there. I looked again and finally recognized her – at least, I deduced that the frail body slumped unattended in a chair at the centre table had to be her. There was a bowl of set, cold porridge in front of her. I said, 'Hello.' She gripped my hand. Her mouth was too dry for her to speak even if she had realized who I was. I sat her up, got some more pillows, made her comfortable, got her a drink and we just sat there. The drugs trolley came round. A measure of something was placed on the table next to the porridge; 'Can you get her to take that?' There was no way. She had no energy even to sip her orange juice. After about half an hour, during which I talked a great deal, filled her in on family news, though she appeared not even to know I was there, she turned, she focused her eyes and she looked at me. For some time we remained eye to eye in silence. I can't explain what she was trying to communicate but I felt I understood. Certainly this supposedly senile old woman left me in no doubt that she knew exactly what was happening to her. As one of the characters says in the play: 'That we should come to this.' But I believe there was more to that look than that. There was an anger and a questioning. An anger in the face of the things we dared not say, an anger born out of frustration for subjects that we had never dared to broach, for feelings and thoughts that could no longer be put into words. My play is an attempt to address that silence.

I've set the play in Birmingham because that is the place and those are the people that I know best. It could be any Midlands town. The people are united by a flatness of speech and by the dryness of their humour. It's worth noting that there is no one Birmingham accent. It varies from one side of town to the other, from one community to another. In particular, out of the characters in this play, only Mrs Jackson would speak with what would be regarded as a strong accent. I'm sure the three sisters would consider themselves to have no accent at all. Upwardly mobile in Birmingham always used to mean, get rid of your accent! Even my grandmother who lived the whole of her married life in a modest inner-city Victorian house with no mod cons – not even hot water – affected a rather grand middle-class manner of speaking.

Having gone on about my grandmother, I should stress that I don't regard this as a play about my family. In fact the characters are drawn from many different sources. My intention was to write about a general condition. The play should be funny, not because that's the way I've contrived it, but because that's the way people are.

STEPHEN BILL

Curtains was first performed at the Hampstead Theatre, London, on 3 September 1987. The cast was as follows:

IDA (aged 86)	Gwen Nelson
KATHERINE (aged 53)	Bridget Turner
GEOFFREY (aged 63)	Ralph Nossek
MICHAEL (their son, aged 30)	Philip Bird
MARGARET (aged 50)	Sheila Ballantine
DOUGLAS (aged 48)	Alfred Lynch
SUSAN (aged 43)	Gillian Hanna
MRS JACKSON (aged 70)	Stella Moray
Director	Stuart Burge
Designer	Tim Reed
Lighting	Nick Chelton

The play is set in the present in the rear living room of an inner-city Victorian house.

ACT ONE

SCENE ONE: LATE AFTERNOON

*An inner-city, Victorian, villa-type house. The rear living room.
Afternoon. The room hasn't been properly redecorated for at least
thirty years, though attempts have been made here and there to brighten
things up. One wall has a few strips of wallpaper on it and the kitchen
door has been painted or half-painted several times. The furniture
similarly reflects the fashions of the last eighty years, though most of it
is pre-war. The light is fairly dingy. There are a lot of photographs
covering several generations of family and there are quite a lot of
ornaments and pictures. There are two doors: one to the hallway and
one to the kitchen. The table is laid for a buffet birthday tea.*

    KATHERINE *and* MARGARET, *sisters in their early fifties, late
forties, respectively, crouch either side of* IDA's *wheelchair.* IDA, *their
mother, tiny and frail, sits propped up with cushions, completely in her
own world. Presents are piled on her lap.* GEOFFREY *and*
MICHAEL, *father and son, watch the opening of the gifts.*
DOUGLAS, *the other son-in-law, bearded and scruffier looking than*
GEOFFREY, *rummages in an old biscuit tin full of nails, screws, fuses
and junk.* MARGARET *opens a card and a present for* IDA.

MARGARET: Oh and what's this? This one's from Jamie and Sue
    and baby John . . .

IDA: Where's Michael?

MICHAEL: I'm here.

KATHERINE: We're all here, Mom.

MARGARET: All the family, just for your birthday; you see how
    we care?

IDA: What day is it?

MARGARET: It's your birthday!

IDA: How quickly it's Friday.

KATHERINE: It's not Friday, Mom.
    (*They laugh.*)

MICHAEL: Do you want to open it then – your present?

KATHERINE: I wonder what it is.

MARGARET: (*aside to* KATHERINE) Towels.
    (*She starts to open the parcel for* IDA)

KATHERINE: Ah . . .

MARGARET: I got them. There's no decent shops at the base.
Oh look, Mom, what's this? Towels, how splendid!

GEOFFREY: Those are nice.

MARGARET: Douglas . . .

DOUGLAS: (*Not looking up*) Great!

KATHERINE: Marks and Sparks?

MARGARET: Oh yes.

KATHERINE: Aren't they lovely, Mom?

MARGARET: Any more? What are you doing, Douglas?

DOUGLAS: (*With hammer and nail*) Putting the thermometer up.

MARGARET: Not now!

DOUGLAS: If I can find a solid enough bit of wall.
(*Front door shuts.*)

MARGARET: Ahh . . . who's this?
(MRS JACKSON *looks round the door.*)
Ah, it's Mrs Jackson! Come in . . .
(*She does so. She is about seventy.*)

IDA: Where? Who's that?

MARGARET: Mrs Jackson.

MRS JACKSON: I've brought you a card, Ida. (*To the family*) Is
she behaving herself?

MARGARET: Oh yes, we're having a lovely birthday, aren't we,
Mom? Shall I open it for you?

DOUGLAS: Where do you want it?

MARGARET: Oh Mom, where do you want the thermometer?

MRS JACKSON: What's that?

GEOFFREY: It's a thermometer.

MRS JACKSON: Oh . . .

MICHAEL: A present from Mom and Dad.

GEOFFREY: Well, we thought . . .

KATHERINE: They're advising all the old people to get them.

MRS JACKSON: What for?

MARGARET: It'll be useful, won't it, Mom?

MRS JACKSON: We had one once, told you the weather.

KATHERINE: Oh . . . This is a special one. Tells you when to
turn the fire up.

MRS JACKSON: Ohh . . .

2

DOUGLAS: (*Holding it against the wall*) There do you?

MARGARET: Not in a draught, Douglas.

DOUGLAS: In this house?

GEOFFREY: After last winter we thought . . .

MARGARET: That was hypothermia, that was.

MRS JACKSON: Her blood's like water, you see, Margaret.

DOUGLAS: There, Mom?

IDA: No.

DOUGLAS: There?

IDA: No.

GEOFFREY: Up a bit I think. (*To* MRS JACKSON) If you or
    Michael could keep an eye on it, if ever you're round . . .

MRS JACKSON: I'm here all the time!

DOUGLAS: There?

MARGARET: What do you think, Mom?

IDA: Down.

MARGARET: Down a bit, Douglas.

IDA: Over there.

MICHAEL: Over there, Douglas.

DOUGLAS: Better?

IDA: Up a bit.

KATHERINE: Oh, mom!
    (*They all laugh.*)

MARGARET: Up a bit, Douglas, all right?

IDA: No; down!

ALL: (*Together*) Down a bit, Douglas!

MARGARET: Oh dear!
    (*Much hilarity.*)

KATHERINE: How's that then, Mom?

IDA: What is it?

ALL: (*Together*) Oh no!

MARGARET: It's a thermometer! Oh I don't know! 'What is it?'!
    (IDA *smiles and shakes her head, bemused.* DOUGLAS *fixes the
    thermometer to the wall.*)

KATHERINE: (*With* MRS JACKSON's *card*) Shall I open this for you?
    (*She does so.*)

MARGARET: How's she been?

MRS JACKSON: Don't ask.

3

KATHERINE: Another card, Mom, aren't you lucky!
　　(*Reads:*) 'May this special day be the best,
　　　　　　　Full of hope and fun.
　　　　　　　And lots of happiness come your way,
　　　　　　　For many years to come.'
MARGARET: Ahh . . .
KATHERINE: (*Reads*) Love, Dora . . .
GEOFFREY: That's nice. And everyone's remembered . . .
MARGARET: (*Aside to* KATHERINE) There's nothing from you-know-who.
KATHERINE: No.
MARGARET: And nothing last Christmas . . .
KATHERINE: Terrible.
MARGARET: (*To* DOUGLAS) Nothing from you-know-who . . .
DOUGLAS: So? Shall we eat then?
MICHAEL: Good idea.
MARGARET: Are you hungry, Mom?
IDA: No, dear.
KATHERINE: Haven't you had some lovely things? Don't forget the bowl of fruit and the gloves . . .
MARGARET: Those were from all of us at High Meadows.
IDA: Lovely. Can you smell the shit?
　　(*All are momentarily speechless.*)
MARGARET: Sorry, Mom; say again?
DOUGLAS: Don't ask her to repeat it.
KATHERINE: I think she said, 'Can you smell the ships?'
MARGARET: Ahh . . . she thinks Jamie's in the navy! No – he's in the air force, Mom, like Douglas was! He flies planes, ha ha! Not the Navy!
　　(*They all laugh.* IDA *is confused.*)
MICHAEL: And he's not coming because he's in the Middle East.
IDA: Poor horse.
KATHERINE: Horse?
IDA: He didn't deserve that.
KATHERINE: Didn't he? (*Looks around for help*) Who's this, Michael?
MICHAEL: Don't ask me, Mother, but if you go out of the back door remember to step over him.

4

KATHERINE: Who?

MICHAEL: The horse! He's been lying there for six weeks now, hasn't he, Granma?

IDA: What dear?

MICHAEL: The horse is dead, isn't he?

IDA: He didn't deserve that!

MICHAEL: No! (*To the others*) Don't worry, she thinks she's in the House of Lords sometimes.

(*He laughs. The others don't understand the joke.*)

KATHERINE: Would you like a bit of tea, Mom?

IDA: Is that her?

KATHERINE: Yes, Mom, it's me . . .

IDA: No!

MARGARET: You must, Mom, it's your birthday!

MRS JACKSON: Well, I'll just . . .

(*She starts to go.*)

MARGARET: Oh no, Mrs Jackson, you must have a bit of the cake at least. Don't go . . .

MRS JACKSON: Oh well . . . I don't like to intrude . . . (*Stays.*) I'm gasping for a cup of tea, Michael.

MICHAEL: Oh . . .

GEOFFREY: Ah yes!

DOUGLAS: I'll put the kettle on.

(*He goes.*)

KATHERINE: Sandwich, anyone?

(*They all start to eat.*)

MARGARET: I've used Dream Topping, did I tell you, for the trifle? It's not that I'm being mean but I thought cream might be a little bit rich.

MRS JACKSON: Oh yes.

IDA: What's that?

MARGARET: Nothing, Mom. I've used Dream Topping for the trifle.

IDA: What's she say?

MARGARET: Only . . . I've used Dream Topping for the trifle. I thought double cream might be a bit rich . . .

(IDA *stares at her.*)

MARGARET: I was only saying because I didn't want you to think

5

I was being penny-pinching . . . it's the same price more or
less . . . On the trifle . . . Dream Topping . . . It tastes very
similar . . . (*Not getting through*) Never mind.

IDA: I don't want any.

MARGARET: No? All right.

(*They all eat, except* IDA.)

GEOFFREY: Mm . . . lovely . . .

KATHERINE: Nice bit of cheese, Margaret.

MARGARET: Bit of cheese, Mom?

(*No response.*)

Are you comfy?

IDA: The pain's terrible.

(*They all look at her. She sits staring straight ahead. They eat.*)

KATHERINE: (*Eventually*) Has she had her tablets, Michael?

MRS JACKSON: She's had everything she can until bedtime.

GEOFFREY: Does sitting up not help perhaps?

MRS JACKSON: It's all the same, Geoffrey. It's in her spine, see.

GEOFFREY: If she could keep moving . . .

KATHERINE: Don't be ridiculous.

GEOFFREY: I know, but if she could . . .

MICHAEL: Dad!

GEOFFREY: I mean it's such a pity when she recovered so well
from the surgery . . .

MARGARET: Oh she's doing wonderfully, aren't you, Mom?

KATHERINE: Maybe we should move on to the cake.

GEOFFREY: (*Still eating sandwiches*) Well, hold on . . .

KATHERINE: Just for Mom.

GEOFFREY: Oh.

MARGARET: Douglas!

DOUGLAS: (*Off*) Hold on.

MARGARET: We need the camera.

KATHERINE: Would you like a piece of cake, Mom?

GEOFFREY: Show her the cake, Mike, that'll cheer her up a bit.

MICHAEL: Here you are, Granma . . . (*He hums the Death March
as he carries it round and presents it to her.*) One birthday cake!
What do you think of that?

KATHERINE: There's eighty-six little flowers on it, Mom. I
couldn't get eighty-six candles on, so you see these little

flowers? There's eighty-six of them.

GEOFFREY: Marvellous.

MARGARET: However did you get them on?

MICHAEL: Piece of cake!

KATHERINE: How I counted them I don't know.

(DOUGLAS *returns with teapot.*)

GEOFFREY: Only fourteen more years and you'll get your
telegram from the Queen. That'll be good, won't it, Mother?

IDA: (*Smiles at him*) No.

GEOFFREY: What do you mean, 'no'? You've got to hang on for
your telegram.

DOUGLAS: She'll outlive us all.

GEOFFREY: Of course she will.

MARGARET: Ready, Doug?

MICHAEL: Ready, Granma?

IDA: No.

MRS JACKSON: Is that the only word you know today? Come on,
cheer up. Make an effort – they've all come a long way!

MARGARET: Are you going to blow out the candle, Mom?

GEOFFREY: Big blow.

MICHAEL: Not too big – we don't want you dropping dead in the
icing – we've got to send a bit to Cyprus.

CATHERINE: Isn't he awful?

MICHAEL: On second thoughts – big blow, granma!

(DOUGLAS *takes a photograph.*)

DOUGLAS: (*To* MICHAEL) What are you after; the house?

MICHAEL: Heh?

GEOFFREY: Gentlemen, please!

MARGARET: Wait a minute – we haven't sung Happy Birthday,
have we? Come on! Come on, Doug! (*Starts the singing:*)
'Happy Birthday to you –'
(*They all sing along.* DOUGLAS *takes pictures.*)
Hip hip . . .
(*They do three cheers.*)

MICHAEL: (*To* DOUGLAS) The house is rented . . .

KATHERINE: Now blow, Mom!

MARGARET: Big blow . . .

(IDA *stares at the flickering candle.*)

7

MICHAEL: Go on, you can do it!
(IDA *looks at him blankly, then back at the cake. The faintest of smiles lights her face. She makes to blow. They all help her. The candle is blown out.*)
MARGARET: Hooray!
KATHERINE: Well done.
GEOFFREY: Very well done indeed!
MICHAEL: Speech, speech!
IDA: You're very kind. You're all very . . . I don't know why you bother, you shouldn't, you know.
GEOFFREY: Of course we should! It's our bounden duty!
KATHERINE: Of course.
GEOFFREY: Because we all love you very much!
(IDA *smiles.*)
MARGARET: You see – she's picking up, aren't you?
MRS JACKSON: She's always brighter when there's people here.
GEOFFREY: Really?
MRS JACKSON: Oh yes.
KATHERINE: Piece of cake then, Mom?
MARGARET: Isn't it a lovely cake? Home-made by Katherine.
KATHERINE: (*Cutting*) Here you are . . .
(DOUGLAS *has climbed on a chair back to get a better angle.*)
MARGARET: Have you finished?
DOUGLAS: If you'd keep still!
(*They all freeze except* IDA *who is oblivious to his efforts but aware of the sudden stillness. Taking it as a note of censure she starts to eat her cake.* DOUGLAS *takes his picture.*)
Thank you.
MARGARET: Doesn't it look delicious? Is it Pru Leith?
(IDA *coughs.*)
KATHERINE: Same recipe as last year.
(IDA *chokes.*)
Are you all right, Mom?
(*She isn't.*)
MRS JACKSON: Oh dear; cough it up! Give her a drink. Did you put too much in, did you?
MARGARET: Is that blood?
MICHAEL: Blood?

8

DOUGLAS: (*Put off his food*) Do you mind?

KATHERINE: Just cake I think. A bit of fondant, was it, Mom?
(IDA *gags again.*)
Oh dear . . .

MARGARET: Are you all right?

MRS JACKSON: Drink this tea.
(*They all watch and wait. Eventually* IDA *recovers.*)

KATHERINE: Has she had any more trouble with the um . . .

MICHAEL: The ulcer?

KATHERINE: The tummy. I mean they don't know, do they,
that she definitely has umm . . .

MICHAEL: How can they? Unless she goes in and has the old
camera stuck down her throat, of course they don't know for
certain, but the evidence . . .

KATHERINE: Better now, Mom?

MRS JACKSON: Too much! She's not eating really, you see.

MICHAEL: Not unless you force her.

MARGARET: She must eat. I wish I could be here more often.
Oh dear. She shouldn't be on her own.

MRS JACKSON: Well, we do what we can.

MARGARET: Oh Mrs Jackson, you're marvellous!

MRS JACKSON: I'm here more or less all the time! But I've got
my own house, you see, to keep tidy and I've only got one
pair of hands . . .

GEOFFREY: Of course!

KATHERINE: It's not satisfactory really.

MRS JACKSON: No it isn't. You see, when I'm watching *Young
Doctors* of an afternoon, I can't hear a thing, so even if she
knocked on the wall . . .

MICHAEL: If she needed a doctor, say . . . Ha ha!

MRS JACKSON: What?

MARGARET: I'm very much afraid that we can't avoid the big
question any longer . . .

DOUGLAS: She's not deaf, you know.

MARGARET: Sorry?

DOUGLAS: We've been over all this before! (*He goes out to the
kitchen.*)

MARGARET: Douglas . . . Now where's he going? (*Calls:*) Don't

9

go spending all afternoon in the garden, Douglas! I know him . . .

IDA: Who was that?

MARGARET: Only Douglas.

IDA: Is that the doctor?

MARGARET: No, it's Douglas.

IDA: Who?

GEOFFREY: How's the farm coming along?

MARGARET: Oh it's going very well. The farm's coming along now, Mom. You'll have to come and see it, won't you?

IDA: No, dear.

MARGARET: You must. Douglas has worked so hard, and . . . (IDA *is looking the other way.* MARGARET *gives up.*)

GEOFFREY: He's settled to it now, has he?

MARGARET: Oh yes.

GEOFFREY: No more . . .

MARGARET: No no!

GEOFFREY: Itchy feet?

MARGARET: No, he's fine. It's a very big responsibility, of course.

GEOFFREY: Well, after service life . . .

MARGARET: Oh he's used to responsibility . . .

GEOFFREY: Oh yes. I was thinking more that after living at the very limits of experience, the sheer excitement of . . . I mean if I was a Red Arrow . . .

KATHERINE: They retire them so young, don't they?

GEOFFREY: Well, it must be very difficult . . .

MARGARET: He's fine.

KATHERINE: Good, we knew he would be.

GEOFFREY: Oh yes.

KATHERINE: And it's such a beautiful spot. You'll have to go, Mom, to the farm.

IDA: Mrs Jackson . . .

MRS JACKSON: Oh . . . I think she wants . . . all right!

KATHERINE: Shall I?

MRS JACKSON: No, I'll see to her, you get your teas. Come on . . . (*Wheeling her out*) You want to do one, do you?

IDA: (*Off*) I want to spit.

MRS JACKSON: (*Off*) Well, you could spit in there! It's only your family. What do you think serviettes are for? I don't know . . . (*They listen.*)

MARGARET: What are we going to do?

MICHAEL: There's a new home just . . .

KATHERINE: No.

MICHAEL: It's supposed to be brilliant.

KATHERINE: 'Katherine, promise me you'll never have me put away.'

MARGARET: It's the workhouse to them.

MICHAEL: Not nowadays.

MARGARET: To them it is.

MICHAEL: Fair enough, if you've got the choice, but surely now we have no choice, I mean Fairlawns is a . . .

KATHERINE: You have to be able to stand up to get in there.

MICHAEL: The Lavenders. Now that is . . .

KATHERINE: Not for the incontinent.

GEOFFREY: A hospice . . .?

KATHERINE: You have to have cancer, something terminal . . .

MICHAEL: Life's terminal! What do you . . .

GEOFFREY: Don't the Council do . . .

KATHERINE: I'm sorry, but no; I couldn't do it!

MARGARET: It killed Doug's mother.

KATHERINE: Right. Just moving them at all, it disorientates them, we know that, Geoffrey . . .

MARGARET: If only I didn't have to go shopping! I mean when I go to Sainsbury's it's a half day at least, this is the problem of living, you know . . . and I couldn't ask Doug and she couldn't be left . . .

KATHERINE: It'll have to be us.

GEOFFREY: Oh no.

MARGARET: No . . .

KATHERINE: What else?

GEOFFREY: I'm sorry, I won't allow it.

MICHAEL: You've tried it once.

KATHERINE: Maybe next time . . .

GEOFFREY: Never again.

KATHERINE: The carpets were new then . . .

MARGARET: Shh . . .

GEOFFREY: She didn't want to be there! She hated it! And took every disgusting opportunity to tell us so. So what's the point? You nearly killed each other!

MARGARET: Shh . . .

(IDA *is wheeled back in.*)

Better, Mom? Are you having a nice birthday? Would you like a little holiday soon, Mom, heh? Where would you really like to go? Tell us and we'll . . . ummm . . .

IDA: I'm going to America, dear.

MARGARET: Oh . . .

GEOFFREY: Ah . . .

MRS JACKSON: You've been listening to Michael, you have! You have some barmy ideas sometimes.

MARGARET: You wouldn't like a bit of country air?

IDA: She nearly killed him!

KATHERINE: That's me, she means.

IDA: An hour there and an hour back – all that travelling just to live in the middle of nowhere! Blooming snob! She should think of her husband! It'll kill him! He has to go to work every day!

MARGARET: They're very happy, aren't you?

GEOFFREY: I've been asked to stand for the Parish Council next year.

MARGARET: How marvellous! Will you?

GEOFFREY: I suppose I should do my duty really.

(DOUGLAS *comes in with an old hand mower.*)

MRS JACKSON: Aye aye . . .

MARGARET: Douglas!

DOUGLAS: Heh?

MARGARET: What on earth . . .

DOUGLAS: Have you seen the back lawn?

MARGARET: Not in here!

DOUGLAS: You said you didn't want me to spend the afternoon in the garden.

MICHAEL: (*Referring to the mower*) What's the problem?

DOUGLAS: Lack of use. (*Sorts through the toolbox.*) Your duties obviously don't extend to lawn care.

MICHAEL: If it had a motor . . .

DOUGLAS: You're supposed to be the motor.

KATHERINE: Have you been in the garden at all, Mom?

MRS JACKSON: Oh no.

MARGARET: Douglas is going to cut the grass for you, isn't that good?

KATHERINE: You must get out there, because you love the garden, don't you?
(*No response.*)

MARGARET: When he's mowed you'll be able to go out there, won't you?
(*No response.*)
Have you had enough to eat? No one's touched the trifle . . . Haven't you had a nice lot of cards? Are you enjoying your birthday? Look at all your cards . . . Anyone know any games?

KATHERINE: Does she want to recite her poems?

MARGARET: Oh yes! Come on, Mom . . . what about all your old poems!

KATHERINE: 'The cottage was a thatched one . . .' How does it go?

MARGARET: (*To* MRS JACKSON) She knows them all by heart, you know . . .

MRS JACKSON: Oh, I know . . .
(*They all watch and wait. No response from* IDA. DOUGLAS *is finding a spanner that fits the mower.* MICHAEL *and* GEOFFREY *watch.*)

MICHAEL: It'll never cut.

GEOFFREY: You'll have to readjust the blades . . .

DOUGLAS: That's what I'm doing.

GEOFFREY: Ah . . . Unless they're finely adjusted it rips at the roots, doesn't it?

MICHAEL: A fine cut is what you want. A good even . . . Shall I hold that?

GEOFFREY: Are you sure that's the right spanner?

DOUGLAS: No.

GEOFFREY: Ah . . .

MARGARET: Is it no good?

MICHAEL: Rusty.

KATHERINE: Can't you do it?

GEOFFREY: See that little nut?

KATHERINE: Oh dear.

MRS JACKSON: It's had no use, has it?

> (*All attention is on the mower.* IDA *stares into space.* DOUGLAS *gets out a small can of oil.*)

GEOFFREY: A little oil, that's it.

MICHAEL: Oil should do it.

MARGARET: Right. It just needs oiling, doesn't it?

GEOFFREY: Try that now.

MICHAEL: That should do it.

MARGARET: It'll be fine now.

> (*The nut is stuck.*)

Oh dear . . .

GEOFFREY: That appears to be stuck.

MRS JACKSON: It's had it, hasn't it?

KATHERINE: She must have had it donkey's years.

MARGARET: Nothing lasts forever, does it?

GEOFFREY: What about if you . . .

> (*The bell rings.*)

MARGARET: Oh . . .

MRS JACKSON: Oh who's that, I wonder?

GEOFFREY: Jehovah's Witnesses, I expect! Blooming nuisance! There's a lot to be said for living in the country.

MICHAEL: I'd better . . .

MRS JACKSON: I'll get it.

> (*She goes.*)

MICHAEL: The vicar's here, Granma . . .

IDA: Oh.

KATHERINE: Don't tease her. He's teasing you!

> (*A lull. They listen.*)

MARGARET: I wonder who . . .

MICHAEL: Are you expecting anyone, Granma? Ha ha . . .

MRS JACKSON: (*Puts her head round the door.*) Umm er . . .

> (*Comes in and shuts the door.*) It's Susan . . .
> (*They all look at her in amazement.*)
> It is . . . It's Susan . . . your Susan . . . Shall I say,

'Come in'? I didn't know what to do, so I just said . . .

GEOFFREY: Susan?

IDA: Who's that?

MARGARET: Nobody, Mom.

KATHERINE: It can't be our Susan?

MRS JACKSON: Yes!

MARGARET: Oh no, what on earth . . .

KATHERINE: Oh dear . . .

(*No one knows what to do. Eventually there is a knock on the door.*)

SUSAN: (*Off*) Hello . . .

MARGARET: No, Doug! Doug . . . it could kill her . . .

KATHERINE: Geoffrey . . .

SUSAN: (*Off*) Mom . . .

(*She looks in. She doesn't expect to see them all there.*) Oh my God . . . Well, well, well . . . (*Silence as she looks around taking in the faces.*) Katherine . . . Margaret . . . Douglas . . .

DOUGLAS: Hello, stranger.

SUSAN: Geoffrey . . . What's all this then, a party?

(*She looks at* IDA *who appears to be in her own world.* SUSAN, *the youngest daughter, is in her early forties.*)

MARGARET: It's Mother's birthday.

SUSAN: Oh, I know, I know . . . Hello, Mom.

IDA: What?

MARGARET: Susan . . .

SUSAN: What?

MARGARET: She's . . . listen; she's not well at all . . .

SUSAN: I know.

(SUSAN *stands looking at her mother. The others exchange glances.*)

MARGARET: Beg pardon?

SUSAN: I know.

MARGARET: Oh . . . well . . . How did you know?

SUSAN: I just knew. Sorry to take you all by surprise. I knew, and I knew I had to come. Mom . . . it's Susan . . .

IDA: Who's that?

SUSAN: It's Susan, I've come to see you. I've brought you some flowers. Happy Birthday!

IDA: Who is it, Mrs Jackson?

MRS JACKSON: Um . . . well, it's Susan . . . you know . . .
    your . . . youngest, your daughter.

IDA: No.

MRS JACKSON: It is. You remember!

IDA: (*No recognition*) Do I? Right . . .

MARGARET: You see? She won't take it in.

SUSAN: It's Susan, Mom . . .
    (*No reaction.*)
    Sorry, I didn't mean to break up the party. Carry on . . .
    (*No one does.*)
    Please . . .

GEOFFREY: Well, so . . . well . . . Where have you just
    umm . . . come from, now . . . were you . . .

SUSAN: Shepton Mallet.

GEOFFREY: Shepton Mallet.

SUSAN: Somerset.

GEOFFREY: I know it, yes . . . very umm . . .

DOUGLAS: You're living there now, are you?

SUSAN: I'm squatting really. My daughter lives there.

DOUGLAS: Ah, I see . . .

SUSAN: How about you?

DOUGLAS: Oh . . .

SUSAN: Still in the Air Force?

DOUGLAS: No, no . . . I'm . . .

MARGARET: He's a farmer now.

SUSAN: A farmer, wow! A farmer in the family now, heh Mom?
    (*No response.*)

MARGARET: She was just beginning to brighten up a bit. Never
    mind . . . Katherine, should we . . .?

KATHERINE: Has she had enough to eat?

MARGARET: I think so.
    (*She gets up.* KATHERINE *follows her lead.*)

MRS JACKSON: What are you doing, shall I . . .?

MARGARET: We can manage, thank you, Mrs Jackson.

SUSAN: What's happening?

MARGARET: She gets very tired.

SUSAN: So? Look, I'd like to sit with her, spend a little time . . .

MARGARET: She hasn't a clue who you are.

KATHERINE: Mom . . .

IDA: Who's that?

KATHERINE: Katherine.

IDA: Who is it?

KATHERINE: It's me, Katherine . . .

IDA: Oh, Margaret! Ohh, she's a cruel woman your sister!

MARGARET: She's not!

SUSAN: Mom . . .

IDA: Who's that?

MARGARET: Well . . .

SUSAN: It's Susan. Mom, I've come to say hello.
(*Silence.* IDA *struggles with her memory.*)

IDA: No . . . I'm sorry, dear. I have too much pain.

MARGARET: You see? Oh dear, it's too much for her this.
I'm sorry, but this is too much.

SUSAN: She's in pain?

KATHERINE: Well, uncomfortable . . .

MARGARET: Mom, would you like to lie down? Mom, shall we
get you into bed?

IDA: No, get off!

MRS JACKSON: It's the getting her in, the moving that hurts
most, you see.

MARGARET: This is ridiculous.

KATHERINE: Is it too late to ring the doctor, Mrs Jackson?

MRS JACKSON: He only saw her last week.

KATHERINE: Well . . . I mean, I don't care if he saw her . . .
Oh dear, I wish we lived nearer . . .

MRS JACKSON: You're supposed to make an appointment
anyway.

MARGARET: What?

MRS JACKSON: I mean, this isn't an emergency, is it? He might
come out tomorrow.

SUSAN: How long has she been in pain?

MARGARET: Oh . . .

KATHERINE: Oh, we . . . Mrs Jackson? We're not here, you
see . . .

MICHAEL: It depends how doped up she is really.

KATHERINE: What's the doctor's name?

MRS JACKSON: Which doctor?

MICHAEL: Witch doctor! Ha!

MRS JACKSON: What? Well, you never know who you're going to get! If you don't mind who comes you could try ringing. The black one's the best.

KATHERINE: What's his name?

MRS JACKSON: I call him Dr Mucky-bee, but I don't know if that's correct. He will come out. The others are useless. (*Goes to the sideboard.*) I've got the number over here. (SUSAN *meanwhile crouches beside her mother.*)

SUSAN: Hello, Mom. How are you? (*She kisses her. They hold hands.*)

MARGARET: Right then . . .

MRS JACKSON: I'm sure he won't come.

KATHERINE: He will, this is ridiculous. I'll phone him.

MARGARET: I'll come with you. Mom, we're just going in the other room to phone the doctor. We're not leaving you. We won't be a second. (*They go out of the room.*)

SUSAN: Well . . .

GEOFFREY: Arthritis of the spine, you see. Very painful. I get a little bit of umm . . . I know . . .

MICHAEL: She had an operation last year, didn't you, Granma?

SUSAN: Did you?

GEOFFREY: Oh yes; she broke her hip – made a hundred per cent recovery – at her age!

MICHAEL: You did well, didn't you, in hospital?

IDA: (*Horrified*) Ohh!

MICHAEL: That's woke her! Ha!

GEOFFREY: She could in fact walk now if she wanted to. It's marvellous what they can do nowadays. The anaesthesia's so good, you see.

MICHAEL: In fact she's nearly all plastic. By the time you get your telegram, Granma, you'll only need the occasional oil and battery change, heh?

IDA: Worst experience of my whole life! I've never been ill in my life!

GEOFFREY: The hospital routine was a bit of an affront to her dignity.

IDA: Wicked people. Never again. Oh no! (*Realizing she is holding a hand.*) Who's this, Mrs Jackson?

MRS JACKSON: Susan. Your Susan. She's come home. To see you.

IDA: No. (*Looks at* SUSAN.) Oh dear, they are liars, you know.

SUSAN: It is me, Susan. (*Shakes her head.*) Aren't you pleased to see me?

(IDA *looks away.*)

MICHAEL: It takes an awful long time for the cogs to grind, you know?

MRS JACKSON: I'll put these in water. Do you remember Michael then?

SUSAN: I'd never have . . .

MICHAEL: No.

(MRS JACKSON *takes some of the tea things out to the kitchen.*)

SUSAN: And you look older, Douglas. In fact I don't think I would have recognized anyone, Mom . . . He's still as handsome, Mom, isn't he, Douglas? I looked out for you during the Falklands fiasco.

DOUGLAS: For me?

MICHAEL: Jamie was there.

DOUGLAS: My son. Bloody madness!

SUSAN: And now they're drilling for oil.

GEOFFREY: Are they really?

SUSAN: How they deceive us.

GEOFFREY: Well umm . . . well . . .

SUSAN: What?

MICHAEL: Take no notice.

(SUSAN's *attention goes back to* IDA *who is staring in the opposite direction.*)

SUSAN: All right, Mom? I should have let you know I was coming, sorry, Mom, but I didn't know what to say and it was all very last minute.

IDA: What's going on, dear, do you know?

SUSAN: Well . . . where should I begin? It's your birthday, right? And do you remember, Mom, your youngest daughter, Susan?

IDA: Who's this?

SUSAN: This is Susan.

IDA: I don't know anything any more, dear. I've had enough, I know that. Who are you?

SUSAN: Susan. The one that went away.

IDA: I know; you did!

SUSAN: Right! I was a naughty girl!

(IDA *just looks at her.*)

Well, I wasn't all bad, I married the chap, you'll be pleased to know, when he finally got divorced. We had two children, then we went our different ways . . . then I had another little girl, well, she's a big girl now. I've seen the world, Mom, you know? And now I've come back. I dreamt about you last night; you were poorly. My daughter woke me. She said, 'Mom, you're crying.' I thought I'd better come home. Ow . . .

(IDA *is gripping her hand tightly.*)

You've lost none of your strength, have you?

DOUGLAS: Twenty-five years.

SUSAN: That's right.

(*She and* DOUGLAS *stare at each other for some time.*)

A long time. It was amazing walking back up the road.

GEOFFREY: Oh dearie me, yes! It's changed, hasn't it?

SUSAN: I was amazed by how much hadn't changed. I passed houses with the same vase in the window as when I was a child. The same colour paintwork. I don't think it has changed, Geoffrey.

GEOFFREY: Well . . .

MRS JACKSON: Did you see any white faces?

SUSAN: I saw a lot of children. That was nice. And they've made it a one-way street . . .

MICHAEL: The traffic's ridiculous.

GEOFFREY: It's gone right down. Michael lives here, he knows.

SUSAN: You live here?

MICHAEL: I keep an eye on Granma.

DOUGLAS: Saves himself a fortune in rent.

MICHAEL: It's handy for the university.

GEOFFREY: He works, you see, in umm . . .

DOUGLAS: I bet you could do with a drink.

SUSAN: I could.

DOUGLAS: Have you got any drink in, Michael?

MICHAEL: Ginger wine?

DOUGLAS: We bought that for her last Christmas. Oh, go on then.

SUSAN: This room . . .

GEOFFREY: We've offered to decorate, haven't we, Doug?

SUSAN: Extraordinary . . .

DOUGLAS: How did you get here?

SUSAN: Sorry?

DOUGLAS: Not by car then?

SUSAN: I don't have a car.

DOUGLAS: Train.

SUSAN: Bus.

DOUGLAS: Bus . . .

SUSAN: I've got some pictures in my bag . . .

GEOFFREY: She can't see.

SUSAN: Oh.

DOUGLAS: Only shapes. She knows you're there, but the detail has gone.

SUSAN: (*Holds* IDA's *hand to her face.*) Oh . . .
   (MICHAEL *pours drinks.* MRS JACKSON *returns with the flowers.*)

MRS JACKSON: Here you are. Don't they look nice? Ida, she's bought you some flowers, so say thank you very much. Flowers cost the earth these days.

SUSAN: Can I? (*Takes the vase from* MRS JACKSON.)
   Here, Mom, smell . . .

IDA: Roses.

SUSAN: Yes! It's a yellow one. Have you still got that yellow rose by the back door?

DOUGLAS: Margaret tidied it all up last year.

MICHAEL: It's gone, that has.

SUSAN: These are from my daughter's garden. The perfume's so strong, isn't it? It always reminds me of here. Whenever we walked past it you'd always say, 'Here, smell this.'
   (IDA *smiles and tries to grasp a bloom.*)
   Mind the thorns . . .

21

(IDA *tries very hard to hold a flower but no longer has the control.*)
Careful, they're a bit delicate now, with all the travelling . . . Can you smell? Remember that time . . .
(*A door shuts in the hallway.*)

GEOFFREY: Ahh . . .

SUSAN: What's that?

(MARGARET *and* KATHERINE *return.*)

MRS JACKSON: Did you get through?

MARGARET: Oh yes.

KATHERINE: And do you know what the doctor said?

MRS JACKSON: I told you!

IDA: What is it, dear?

SUSAN: Nothing.

MARGARET: What did he say, Katherine? You won't believe this!

KATHERINE: He asked me how old she was. I said, 'She's eighty-six.' He said, 'Oh well then, what do you expect – of course she'll be in pain'!

MARGARET: And he refused to come out. Have you ever heard anything so disgusting?

DOUGLAS: Report him.

KATHERINE: A friend of ours reported her doctor and what happened, Geoffrey?

GEOFFREY: Right; no other doctor in the area would take her on.

MICHAEL: So?

MRS JACKSON: What are you going to do?

(DOUGLAS *goes back to the mower.*)

MARGARET: I'm so angry I can't speak! She was definitely brightening up, wasn't she, Douglas? Douglas! (*He ignores her.*) Look at all this food!

MRS JACKSON: Blooming doctors!

GEOFFREY: They don't care, do they?

MICHAEL: Well, I hope when I get to that age . . . If I ever do.

DOUGLAS: The odds are you won't.

MICHAEL: Oh, thank you!

DOUGLAS: Someone's bound to press the little button before then.

SUSAN: Oh, don't.

GEOFFREY: Oh, now, now, let's not be gloomy! I would have thought the odds are that we all will. Our longest period ever without war!

SUSAN: Where do you live?

GEOFFREY: Sorry? Oh, Hampton-in-Arden; do you remember it, a very pleasant little . . . ummm . . .

(SUSAN *shakes her head despairingly. It stops the conversation.*)

KATHERINE: All right, Mom?

MARGARET: Mom . . .

(*No response.*)

Well, I only hope . . .

(*They wait for her to continue. She doesn't.*)

DOUGLAS: What?

MARGARET: Well, it's not in our hands, is it?

GEOFFREY: Absolutely.

DOUGLAS: What isn't? The button? War? Or our lives?

MARGARET: Michael said, 'If ever he gets to that age . . .'

DOUGLAS: I heard him!

MARGARET: And I said, 'It's not in our hands.'

DOUGLAS: Isn't it?

KATHERINE: (*To* SUSAN) Have you had anything to eat?

SUSAN: No.

KATHERINE: Michael . . .

(MICHAEL *passes* SUSAN *a plate and offers her the sandwiches.*)

MICHAEL: Here you are.

SUSAN: Thank you.

(DOUGLAS *tries out the mower. It works. He walks up and down in the very confined space in front of the fire. They all watch.*)

GEOFFREY: Well, that's all right, isn't it?

The rear living room. Evening. KATHERINE *wheels* IDA *in from the kitchen. She is well wrapped up. The daylight is fading but no light is switched on.*

KATHERINE: Bed now?

IDA: No.

KATHERINE: Margaret's in bed. It's very late.

> (KATHERINE *stops one of* IDA's *blankets slipping down.*
> IDA *holds her arm.*)
> A drink?
> (IDA *holds on to the arm.*)
> What do you want? I don't know what you want, Mom . . .

IDA: Oh dear.

KATHERINE: Don't you feel ready for sleep, is that the problem? It's been an exciting day, hasn't it? Wait till I tell everyone you've been in the garden till this time! You want to get Michael to take you out there more often, now the grass is cut . . .

IDA: You promised me . . .

KATHERINE: Hasn't Douglas done a good job? Aren't you lucky . . . It's been a nice day, hasn't it? A nice birthday, yes?

> (*There are tears in* IDA's *eyes.*)
> Mom . . . come on, Mom . . . not today . . . (*Gets her handkerchief.*) Would you like a drink? Has it all been a bit much, has it? I think she just wanted to see you. She should have warned us, shouldn't she? Is that what's upset you?

IDA: You know.

KATHERINE: Look, here's a lemon barley here. This must be yours . . . (*Hands her a glass.*) Here you are. Are you uncomfortable? (*Gets her pills from the wall cupboard.*) As it's your birthday. Just one more . . .

IDA: What's this?

KATHERINE: Your pills.

> (KATHERINE *opens the bottle and puts it in* IDA's *hand.*)
> Is that the right bottle?
> (IDA *stares at* KATHERINE.)
> Oh . . . I, I, I'm going to check the back door, all right?

24

Did I lock it? I'm going to check the back door . . .
(*She heads for the kitchen. She stops by the kitchen door not looking, just waiting.* IDA *starts to cram pills into her mouth,* KATHERINE *turns, sees what she's doing and turns away.* IDA *chokes.*)
Oh my God! Swallow, Mom, swallow! (*Tries to help her.*) Oh God in heaven help me! Drink some juice, drink some juice! (*The pills are spat everywhere as* IDA *chokes.*)
Drink, Mom! I can't do it, Mom, I can't!

IDA: Please!
(KATHERINE *grabs a Sainsbury's plastic bag from the table, tips out the contents and puts it over* IDA's *head. It is too big. She leaves it, turns away, but eventually pulls it off.*)

KATHERINE: Ohh . . .
(*In desperation* KATHERINE *grabs a cushion and puts it over* IDA's *face. She lies her own body across, embracing mother, pillow and chair.*)
Oh God!
(*She remains like that for a considerable length of time. The front door slams.*)
Aghh!
(*She moves and sits on a chair still holding the cushion.* GEOFFREY *comes in.*)

GEOFFREY: Anyone home? No light on . . . (*Switches it on.*) Is she still up?
(*He comes in and sees the pills and bottle on* IDA's *lap.*)
Oh . . . Oh my God . . . Katherine . . . Katherine . . . What the . . . Is she . . . is she?
(KATHERINE *is not listening to him.* GEOFFREY *checks* IDA's *pulse.*)
What are these (*the pills*)? Oh my Lor' . . . Katherine . . .
(*She can't look at him. She remains clutching the cushion.*)
Well . . . (*Lays* IDA's *wrist down.*) Well, I think she's . . .
(KATHERINE *looks at* IDA *for the first time. She goes over to her. She picks up the pills which are all over the blankets and clothes. She props the body up with the cushion.*)
What happened?
(*No reply.*)

25

Katherine? You're shaking . . .

(*Once* IDA *is cleaned up a bit* KATHERINE *kisses her.*)

KATHERINE: Well, that's it.

GEOFFREY: Katherine . . . what happened?

KATHERINE: We'd better lie her down before . . .

GEOFFREY: Before what?

(*No reply.*)

Katherine . . .

(*She starts to push the wheelchair.*)

I don't know whether we should . . .

(KATHERINE *stops and walks away.*)

I mean, I don't know . . . What do you think? I mean you were . . . She does look a little more umm . . . Now you've . . . Did she . . . I mean all those pills she didn't umm . . .

KATHERINE: Geoffrey!

GEOFFREY: Sorry. Sorry but . . . Oh God! Why do these things always happen at night! This is all I need. It was a very long meeting. This I did not bargain for! I'm sorry, I can't think straight. What happened?

KATHERINE: Oh Mom . . .

GEOFFREY: Look, it's all right. I'll call Mrs Jackson, shall I? I mean we can't not do . . . Where is everybody? I'll knock Mrs Jackson . . .

(*No response from* KATHERINE. *He knocks on the wall.*)

She won't hear that, will she? She'll be in bed I expect. I suppose I'd better . . .

(*He heads for the door. There's a knock on the wall.*)

Ahh . . . (*Stops and tries to take stock.*) Right . . . Why don't you just sit down and . . .

(*He sits down and they wait in silence.*)

Where is everybody?

(KATHERINE *shrugs.* GEOFFREY *looks at the body, he looks at* KATHERINE. *He'd like to say something.*)

(*Eventually.*)

We raised a hundred pounds tonight, Somalia I think it's going to . . . Are you all right now? Was it a shock? I mean what happened, tell me?

26

KATHERINE: I don't know! I just, I just . . .

GEOFFREY: What?

KATHERINE: Oh, for God's sake!

GEOFFREY: You just found her like this? I mean how long has
    she . . . I mean I thought she went to bed? It's . . .

KATHERINE: We've been in the garden.

GEOFFREY: At this hour? I mean . . . (*Looks at his watch.*) I
    think I'm going to have to . . . I mean someone has to be
    informed . . . If she . . . I mean, is this what it seems . . .
    I mean, if it is then . . .
    (*The front door slams.*)
    Ahh . . . or has someone already . . .
    (MRS JACKSON *comes in.*)

MRS JACKSON: What is it? Oh dear, I knew, I knew . . . the
    minute you knocked . . . oh dear, yes . . .

GEOFFREY: There's no pulse.

MRS JACKSON: What's she doing up? We'd better lie her down.

GEOFFREY: Should we . . .?

MRS JACKSON: If you don't lie her flat in a minute, you'll never
    lie her flat again!

GEOFFREY: Oh.

MRS JACKSON: (*To* KATHERINE) Never mind dear; a blessed
    release, heh?

KATHERINE: I'll give you a hand.

MRS JACKSON: No! You Just . . .
    (KATHERINE *helps.*)
    All right.
    (*They go out. When they have gone* GEOFFREY *spots the empty
    pill bottle. He picks it up and reads it. Realizing what he's done,
    he puts it down, then picks it up and wipes it thoroughly. He puts
    it back where he found it. A few moments later he moves it and
    places it behind a picture. He starts to leave the room, hesitates
    and returns once again to the bottle. He removes some rubbish
    from the waste-paper basket, picks the bottle up with a scrap of
    serviette and drops it in the basket. Then he casually drops the
    waste-paper back in covering up the bottle.* KATHERINE *returns*
    en route *for the kitchen.*)

GEOFFREY: Has anyone been informed?

KATHERINE: Mrs Jackson's phoning the doctor.

GEOFFREY: Ah . . . I was wondering . . .

KATHERINE: (*Stops, waiting for him to continue*) What?

GEOFFREY: I'm not sure, I mean, I don't know, whether we've done the right thing.

(KATHERINE *looks at him.*)

Moving her. You're looking a bit better now, your colour's coming back. What does Mrs Jackson think?

(KATHERINE *comes and sits down, prepared to talk to him.*)

She didn't seem to me to bat an eyelid. I think it's possible that it never crossed her mind that it was anything other than . . . I mean once you'd tidied her up she did look just . . . I mean, maybe . . . who knows, we'll see what the doctor . . . Do you remember with my mother he was in and out in two minutes? It'll only be the night-time relief. Some Iranian refugee . . . It's as well everyone is out of the way. Where is everybody?

KATHERINE: Margaret's in bed.

GEOFFREY: Did Susan go home?

KATHERINE: No.

GEOFFREY: Where is she?

KATHERINE: (*Impatient*) I don't know!

GEOFFREY: And the chaps are at the pub, I suppose . . .

(*No reply. There's a long silence.*)

So . . . How did she come to . . . She'd asked to go in the garden, had she? And what happened? Did you just leave her in here for a while? (*Trying to lighten it.*) Where did all those pills come from? Isn't she a rogue! What did she do, just . . .

KATHERINE: Oh, for God's sake, Geoffrey!

GEOFFREY: I'm sorry, I'm sorry! Weren't there a lot of pills? It looked to me . . . tell me I'm wrong! But I have to know! Heavens, Katherine, when I came in here, if I didn't know you . . .

KATHERINE: What?

GEOFFREY: Shh . . . It's all right; now look everything's fine . . .

(GEOFFREY *goes across to comfort her, she shrugs him off.*

28

MRS JACKSON *comes in.* KATHERINE *goes out to the kitchen.*)

MRS JACKSON: The doctor's on his way. Is she upset? She will be, it's always worse when the second one goes.

GEOFFREY: The second?

MRS JACKSON: When both your parents . . .

GEOFFREY: Oh. How did she look to you, Mrs Jackson?

MRS JACKSON: Not good.

GEOFFREY: Really?

MRS JACKSON: Have you given her a drink?

GEOFFREY: Oh no, no . . . I meant Mother.

MRS JACKSON: (*Looks at him*) Ida? Well, I can't do any more . . .

GEOFFREY: No!

MRS JACKSON: Not till the doctor's been. There's nothing more I can do.

GEOFFREY: No, no quite.

MRS JACKSON: She's at peace now. (*Picks a pill up off the floor.*) Look at this . . . (*Picks another up.*)

GEOFFREY: What's that?

MRS JACKSON: Look at this . . . spits them out, you see. I find them in her pockets, down the bed. (*Collects them.*) If you don't take your pills then what do you expect? Now where's the bottle gone? (*Goes to the wall cupboard to look for the pill bottle.*) That was a new lot, have you seen it?

(GEOFFREY, *for once, is speechless. He stands staring at her.*)

ACT TWO

SCENE ONE: LATE EVENING

The rear living room. Late evening. The sound of the back door shutting. MICHAEL *and* DOUGLAS *come in from the kitchen carrying a few cans.*

MICHAEL: I mean, if we invested one hundred billion now in research we might in ten years be where the Japs are now – and by then, of course, they'll be another ten or twenty years ahead. Why hang about?

DOUGLAS: Have you taken to the streets on this issue? Written to your Honourable Member?

MICHAEL: D'agh! Nobody, nobody, has given me a convincing argument for staying in this country.

DOUGLAS: So where are you going?

MICHAEL: Oh, I'm going!

DOUGLAS: Yes, but where?

MICHAEL: Ah well, this is it . . . this is it!

DOUGLAS: Absolutely!

MICHAEL: I'm going! Anything new over here, they don't want to know! We've been massacred, we have in our department. Funding for about one more year. You can't live like that, you know? It's a mug's game. There's a chap in our department – Ph.D., M.Sc. – brilliant! Pure physicist – he's joined the Inland Revenue, can you believe that? (GEOFFREY *comes in from the hallway.*)

GEOFFREY: Ah . . . ah . . . Michael . . .

MICHAEL: Blimey, are you still here?

GEOFFREY: Shh . . . I'm afraid Mother's umm . . .

MICHAEL: What?

GEOFFREY: She's passed away.

MICHAEL: I've just bought her a Mackeson!

GEOFFREY: Oh dear. Well, I'm sorry, but . . .

MICHAEL: Oh blimey . . . she's dead? On her birthday? Well, that's timing for you!

DOUGLAS: In her sleep, or was it . . . you know?

GEOFFREY: It was umm . . . to be perfectly honest, I don't

know. I wasn't here, you see. So . . . Mrs Jackson's just
woken Margaret. I believe she's got a migraine, is that correct?

DOUGLAS: Oh hell yes, I suppose I'd better . . . (*Sits down.*)
Oh God . . .

MICHAEL: Oh well . . .

GEOFFREY: So . . .

MICHAEL: Are you sure she's dead?

GEOFFREY: What? What do you mean?

MICHAEL: Well, she's looked dead for weeks. I mean, she does
when she's asleep.

GEOFFREY: She has no pulse.

MICHAEL: She hasn't for weeks.

GEOFFREY: Oh, I think she's . . .

MICHAEL: How do you know?

GEOFFREY: Well . . .

MICHAEL: Is Mom with her?

GEOFFREY: Yes.

MICHAEL: I mean it would be terrible if you buried her . . .

GEOFFREY: Michael . . .

DOUGLAS: (*Getting up*) There are procedures! You don't just dig
a hole and bingo!
(*He goes to see* MARGARET.)

GEOFFREY: Exactly. The doctor's been called and that's his job.

MICHAEL: Would you like a Mackeson?

GEOFFREY: No, thank you.

MICHAEL: If she knew the price of these!

GEOFFREY: Shh . . . If you could just . . .

MICHAEL: What? Why are we whispering?

GEOFFREY: I think your mother's quite upset.

MICHAEL: Oh.
(MRS JACKSON *comes in.*)

MRS JACKSON: All right, Michael?

MICHAEL: Well . . . *I'm* all right . . .

MRS JACKSON: It's for the best, I suppose.

MICHAEL: Oh yes. I might even get a night's sleep! I'll just . . .
I suppose I'd better . . .
(*He goes out into the hallway.* MARGARET *can be heard.*)

MARGARET: (*Off*) She was doing so well today!

MRS JACKSON: (*Pulling the door to*) Douglas is with her now.

GEOFFREY: Good, good.

MRS JACKSON: Well, I don't know . . . I think I should tell you, Geoffrey . . . I can tell you, can't I? I don't want to, you know . . .

GEOFFREY: What?

MRS JACKSON: (*Confidentially*) I just popped my head round the door . . .

MARGARET: (*Off*) Ohhh God!

(MICHAEL *comes back in, obviously too embarrassed to remain with* MARGARET.)

MRS JACKSON: (*Very confidentially*) I think I ought to tell you this: your wife, she was right over the bed, I said, 'What are you doing dear?' She was taking pills out of Ida's mouth. I'm sure that's what she was doing. 'I'm just tidying her up,' she said. I can't find the pill bottle anywhere. I can't! I know it was up there. I gave her her last pills . . . I always . . .

MICHAEL: What's that?

GEOFFREY: It's all right, Michael. So what are you umm . . .?

MRS JACKSON: Nothing . . . nothing, nothing . . . I'm not saying anything. But I don't think the doctor will like it if, you know . . . If somebody's been careless enough to leave that bottle where she could get hold of it. I always put it back up there!

MICHAEL: Her pills? That new bottle?

GEOFFREY: No, it's all right, Michael.

MRS JACKSON: I didn't say anything to Katherine.

GEOFFREY: No, no, good . . . I see . . . but you think there's a possibility that . . . you think Ida may have . . . umm . . .

MRS JACKSON: Oh, I don't know!

GEOFFREY: No, no, of course not. Thank you for telling me and I think you're right, I wouldn't say anything to Katherine . . . or Margaret . . . or . . .

MRS JACKSON: Oh no, no I wouldn't!

GEOFFREY: We must be wary of putting two and two together and making six, you know?

MRS JACKSON: Oh, I wouldn't! But I thought I should just warn you, that's all. You don't mind me mentioning it, do you?

GEOFFREY: No, no, thank you.

MICHAEL: What's that then?

MRS JACKSON: It's nothing, dear.

MICHAEL: Have you lost the pill bottle?

GEOFFREY: No, no no!

MICHAEL: They're up here . . . (*Looking in the wall cupboard*)
   I always put them up here . . . Ohh . . .

GEOFFREY: Anyway . . .

MICHAEL: They're not here.

GEOFFREY: Well, we don't need them now, do we?

MICHAEL: They must be somewhere! What did you say Mom
   was doing, Mrs Jackson?

MRS JACKSON: Oh, me?
   (MARGARET *comes in followed by* DOUGLAS.)
   All right, Margaret?

MARGARET: She killed her.

GEOFFREY: What?

MARGARET: I don't care what anyone says; she's killed her! She
   was getting better!

DOUGLAS: No.

MARGARET: She was fine at tea-time – she smiled!

DOUGLAS: Here, sit down . . .

MARGARET: She's killed her, Douglas! Mrs Jackson, wasn't she
   picking up?

MRS JACKSON: Oh, I don't . . . look, dear, I don't think we
   should go putting two and two together . . . and making
   four, you know?

MARGARET: If it wasn't for my sister!

DOUGLAS: Just calm down.

GEOFFREY: Yes, yes; let's just take it easy, shall we?

MARGARET: As soon as she came back, I knew! I knew!

GEOFFREY: Susan?

MARGARET: Yes!

GEOFFREY: Ah . . .

MARGARET: I knew there was something fishy! You see, Mrs
   Jackson, she was the youngest, as you know. She had all the
   advantages we never had and what has she done? Thrown
   her life away!

DOUGLAS: How do you know?

MARGARET: I know! I understand perfectly! Over forty and not
settled down! How many broken marriages? She's realized –
it happens at that age – she's realized her life is a complete
mess. She could have gone to university – the world was her
oyster! Now she's middle-aged, got nothing and is having to
face up to it! But rather than being adult about it and
blaming herself, she's blamed Mother! That's why she's
come back! That or guilt!

MRS JACKSON: But she wouldn't . . .

MARGARET: What?

MRS JACKSON: Oh no, nothing. It's none of my business. That
wouldn't make anyone . . .

MARGARET: What?

(MRS JACKSON *looks to* GEOFFREY *and shrugs.*)
Mark my words, she's killed her, Mrs Jackson, as sure as . . .
(KATHERINE *comes in.*)
A shock like that, at her age!

GEOFFREY: All right?

MARGARET: Can you believe it, Katherine?
(KATHERINE *shakes her head.*)
Nor me. Nor me . . . Where is she?

KATHERINE: Who?

MARGARET: Susan?

KATHERINE: She went out to phone.

MARGARET: Ha! There's a phone here! Gone out to phone . . .
(*They sit in silence. Her head hurts.*)
I could understand it if I'd eaten cheese, but I deliberately
didn't, not even a Dairylea . . . Has someone phoned the
doctor?

GEOFFREY: Oh yes.

MARGARET: Poor, poor Mom . . .

MRS JACKSON: Well . . .

MARGARET: Where was she, when she . . .?

GEOFFREY: In here, I believe.

MARGARET: In here?

KATHERINE: I took her out into the garden. She asked. It was a
beautiful evening. She asked. She asked me to . . .

34

MARGARET: There you are, you see; she was getting better!

DOUGLAS: You don't get better at eighty-six! She was fifty per cent plastic and in terrible pain. You should be thanking God, Margaret – it's a blessed release.

MARGARET: I'm sorry, but oh no . . . I'm sorry, but I can't . . . I can't believe . . . something's not . . . something doesn't . . .

MRS JACKSON: She was suffering, dear.

GEOFFREY: She's at peace now.

MICHAEL: She had had enough, she told me that . . . but . . .

DOUGLAS: What?

MICHAEL: (*After a while*) Have you seen the pills? The bottle?

DOUGLAS: Me?

MICHAEL: Mrs Jackson said . . .

MRS JACKSON: I said nothing, dear.

MICHAEL: Oh well. It's always kept up there – all her medicines are. Have you had it, Mom?

KATHERINE: What? What are you talking about, Michael?

MICHAEL: Nothing . . .

(*Pause. The front door shuts.*)

GEOFFREY: Ah . . . that'll be . . .

MARGARET: She's killed her.

KATHERINE: What?

MARGARET: She has.

KATHERINE: Please, Margaret!

DOUGLAS: Nobody has killed anyone!

(KATHERINE *goes to tell* SUSAN. GEOFFREY *follows.*)

MARGARET: I'm sorry, but you don't sit up and smile and ask to go into the garden one minute, then next minute boompf!

DOUGLAS: You do! I'm sorry but that's life, baby, you do!

MARGARET: Oh no, no, no.

(*They sit listening and waiting.*)

MICHAEL: What were you saying then, Mrs Jackson?

MRS JACKSON: I wasn't, dear.

MICHAEL: Oh.

(SUSAN *comes in with* KATHERINE *and* GEOFFREY.)

SUSAN: Oh well . . . That's a shock.

MARGARET: Where have you been?

35

SUSAN: (*Taken aback*) I'm sorry?

MARGARET: Where have you been?

SUSAN: I've been to make a phone call.

MARGARET: Oh. How many ten pences did that cost you?

SUSAN: What?

MARGARET: It was a long phone call, wasn't it?

(*Silence.* MICHAEL *edges towards the door.*)

MICHAEL: I think I'll just, you know?

(*He goes out to the hallway.*)

SUSAN: It was a short phone call actually. Then I went to look for Douglas and Michael. I must have got the wrong pub.

DOUGLAS: The New Inns.

SUSAN: I went to the Beehive, and the Villa Cross.

MARGARET: You went looking for pubs round here, on your own?

SUSAN: Reclaiming the night, Margaret.

MARGARET: What?

SUSAN: It doesn't matter. How did Mom . . . I mean, what happened?

DOUGLAS: Katherine?

(*They all look to* KATHERINE *who appears on the brink of an explanation. She looks from one to the other. Eventually she shakes her head, unable to speak.*)

SUSAN: It doesn't matter. We're waiting for the doctor then, are we?

(KATHERINE *gets up and walks around, then sits down again. It is a long time before any one speaks. This is the moment when it gets through to them that she is dead.*)

At least she'll have no more pain.

MRS JACKSON: That's right.

SUSAN: At least I saw her. What time did she . . .?

GEOFFREY: Ten, half ten, was it, Katherine? (*No response.*)

SUSAN: Oh, how stupid, stupid! I only went out to a phone so as not to disturb her!

MARGARET: She wasn't asleep. She's been in the garden, she was right as rain!

SUSAN: Oh shit! Shit! Had she forgiven me, do you think, or was this her final revenge! Just when I come home! To leave me

36

just when I needed her, wanted her, wanted to put things right! Sorry, sorry . . . ohh . . . oh Douglas!
(*She puts her arms round* DOUGLAS *and buries her head in his chest. She is upset.*)
Sorry . . . oh hell . . . (*Pulls herself together.*) Sorry.
(*She looks up at him and hugs him.*)
Oh, that's better, that's nice.
Don't let go. Isn't he lovely?
(MARGARET *stares, unable to speak, for some time.*)
MARGARET: Why did you come back?
SUSAN: I'm sorry?
MARGARET: Forgive me, but I find it very difficult to . . .
DOUGLAS: She's just told you if you listened.
MARGARET: (*Looking to* KATHERINE) Has she?
(MICHAEL *comes back in. He remains in the doorway, thinking.*)
SUSAN: (*Quietly*) Oh Douglas, Douglas, Douglas . . .
MRS JACKSON: Shall I put the kettle on?
GEOFFREY: Ah, Mrs Jackson.
MRS JACKSON: I think that's what's called for, don't you?
GEOFFREY: That would be marvellous!
KATHERINE: Thank you, Mrs Jackson. If you wouldn't mind.
MRS JACKSON: Of course not. (*To* KATHERINE) It's a blessed release dear, really it is.
KATHERINE: Yes.
(MRS JACKSON *goes to the kitchen.*)
God . . . I thought she was going to stand around here all night!
(*She walks up and down, then goes out to the hallway.*)
SUSAN: (*To* DOUGLAS) Do you think . . .?
DOUGLAS: What?
SUSAN: (*Shakes her head*) On her birthday.
MARGARET: On her birthday.
DOUGLAS: Someone has a sense of timing somewhere.
SUSAN: She always was neat. The day I come back!
MARGARET: Yes.
SUSAN: My timing has always been impeccable. Appalling, disastrous, but never sloppy – always spot on, one hundred per cent bulls'-eye bad!

(KATHERINE *returns*.)

After all that effort, after coming all this way . . . I never
said goodbye . . .

KATHERINE: I'm sorry.

SUSAN: What?

KATHERINE: I never said goodbye either.
(MICHAEL *grovels under the table.* SUSAN *goes out to the
hallway.*)

SUSAN: I'd better . . .

DOUGLAS: What are you doing, Michael?

MICHAEL: I'm looking for the pill bottle.

KATHERINE: What?

GEOFFREY: Don't worry about that.

MICHAEL: But it has to be here somewhere. It's not in her room.

GEOFFREY: Forget it, Michael, please!

MICHAEL: But if I could find the pill bottle . . .

DOUGLAS: (*Staggered by the irrelevance*) What?

MICHAEL: Heh?

DOUGLAS: It's a bit late for pills now, sunshine! Unless you refer
to pils as in pilsner as in lager – then I'm with you all the
way.

MICHAEL: But . . .

DOUGLAS: Open a can, go on.

MARGARET: Please!

DOUGLAS: Heh?

MARGARET: Show a little respect.

DOUGLAS: What? Listen, your mother, were she able to be in
two places at once, would be the first to pop a cork right
now!

MARGARET: Rubbish! She'd be mortified!

DOUGLAS: Well . . . (*Holding back*) Yes . . . yes . . .
(MICHAEL *is still searching.*)
Michael, for God's sake . . .

MICHAEL: Mrs Jackson said . . .

DOUGLAS: What?

MICHAEL: I'm a bit concerned . . . I mean, I'm a bit, you know,
I mean Mom . . . did umm . . .

KATHERINE: What?

38

MICHAEL: Mrs Jackson umm . . .

MRS JACKSON: (*Off*) What's that?

MICHAEL: Nothing. I mean quite simply . . . umm . . .
I think . . .

DOUGLAS: Are you sure about that?

MICHAEL: What?

DOUGLAS: Why strain the walnut. (*Tapping his head*) A lager
glass is all we need.

MICHAEL: But . . . (MICHAEL *gives up. He looks for a glass.*)

KATHERINE: (*Restless*) Oh dear . . .

MARGARET: Poor Mom.

GEOFFREY: Are you all right, Katherine?

KATHERINE: I'm fine. The doctor's a long time, isn't he?

MARGARET: What do you think she's doing in there?

DOUGLAS: Saying goodbye.

MARGARET: How she's got the nerve! I'm so angry, Katherine!

DOUGLAS: Why?

MARGARET: Why? (*Stares at him.*) Why?

MICHAEL: (*With lager glass*) Here you are.
(MRS JACKSON *peeps round the door.*)

MRS JACKSON: It won't be a minute now. (*She goes.*)

GEOFFREY: That's what we all need – a cup of tea! (*Pause.*)
Well . . . I think we can all take comfort from the fact that
she had a good life, don't you? A long life . . . She always
wanted to end her days here . . . so that was nice, I
think . . . I think . . . yes . . . and now, of course, there's
going to be a bit of sorting out to do, isn't there?

MARGARET: Oh don't! We must look up her policies.

DOUGLAS: She made a will, didn't she?

MARGARET: Yes.

DOUGLAS: That'll make it easier.

MARGARET: Are the step-ladders still under the stairs,
Katherine?

KATHERINE: I don't know.
(MRS JACKSON *comes in with a tea tray.*)

MRS JACKSON: Here we are.

MARGARET: Mrs Jackson, are the step-ladders still under the
stairs?

39

MRS JACKSON: Yes, dear.

MARGARET: Douglas, I want you up in that loft first thing in the morning.

DOUGLAS: What?

MARGARET: I don't think anyone's been up there for years, have they? We'll sort this place out, Katherine, all right? I don't want her . . . She's having nothing.

DOUGLAS: There's nothing to have.

MARGARET: I've a good mind to hide that vase.

DOUGLAS: Somebody should have – years ago!

MARGARET: You might not like it, but there's money in junk! Especially Victorian junk. Do you watch *The Antiques Roadshow*, Katherine?

KATHERINE: Yes. Yes.

MARGARET: Well, you'll know then. If she mentions them, say you're having them.

KATHERINE: What?

MARGARET: The vases. Everything.

KATHERINE: I want nothing!

MARGARET: Neither do I! That little table in the front is nice, you know . . . and that dressing-table set upstairs and the standard lamp. That's real oak, someone must have that.

MRS JACKSON: The three-piece is nice, you know.

MARGARET: You have it, Mrs Jackson.

MRS JACKSON: Oh no!

(KATHERINE *puts her head in her hands.*)

GEOFFREY: All right, dear?

KATHERINE: I'm all right.

MARGARET: I can't believe it, can you, Katherine?

MRS JACKSON: I can't believe it, you know.

MARGARET: She was picking up, wasn't she, Mrs Jackson?

MRS JACKSON: Well . . .

MARGARET: She was.

MRS JACKSON: You never know at that age, dear. She was a good age.

DOUGLAS: What's good about it?

MRS JACKSON: Heh?

DOUGLAS: Nothing.

MRS JACKSON: She had a good life, you know, didn't she? Till these last few years, it was a shame to see really.

(SUSAN *returns*.)

Tea, Susan?

SUSAN: I'd rather have a beer, thank you, or something.

DOUGLAS: Michael . . .

(MICHAEL *gets up to get another glass*.)

Here . . . (DOUGLAS *offers her a can and she drinks from it*.)

MRS JACKSON: Cake, anyone?

SUSAN: No, thank you.

MICHAEL: (*Going to the kitchen*) That's probably what killed her.

MRS JACKSON: It won't keep.

MARGARET: It was extremely light!

SUSAN: Poor Mom. She looks peaceful enough.

MRS JACKSON: She's at rest now, dear.

(MICHAEL *returns with a glass*. SUSAN *doesn't need it*.)

SUSAN: I only wish . . .

DOUGLAS: What?

SUSAN: What's the point of wishing? That's a wonderful picture in there of you (*Douglas*) in your uniform.

DOUGLAS: That old thing.

SUSAN: And with the sports car. Are you still a speed freak?

DOUGLAS: As in miles-per-hour, you mean?

SUSAN: Yes. You look so young in there. Almost how I remember you. (*To* MARGARET) Is he still a mad driver?

(MARGARET *doesn't reply*.)

I'll never forget going round that blind corner with you at ninety miles an hour.

DOUGLAS: When was that?

SUSAN: You don't remember? In that sports car!

DOUGLAS: Oh, the frog-eyed Sprite.

SUSAN: A hundred miles an hour on the wrong side of the road!

DOUGLAS: I don't remember.

SUSAN: You don't remember? My God, it was one of the most extraordinary nights of my life. The same night we drove down the M1 motorway. They'd just opened it. Don't you remember really? A hundred and twenty miles an hour we were doing.

41

MICHAEL: Were there no limits?

SUSAN: God no, there were no limits!

DOUGLAS: And no breathalyser.

MICHAEL: Blooming heck, you can't do anything these days.
(KATHERINE *stands up*.)

MARGARET: Katherine, are you all right?

KATHERINE: I just feel a bit . . .

GEOFFREY: Do you want to lie down?

MARGARET: I should lie down. My migraine, you know? It's
still awful, I can't see. Whole areas are blurred . . . when I
look at you . . .

DOUGLAS: Go to bed.

MARGARET: Don't be silly, Douglas.
(*The door bell rings*.)

KATHERINE: Ahh . . . that'll be . . .

MARGARET: About time too.

MRS JACKSON: Shall I?

GEOFFREY: No, no, it's all right, I'd better . . . I'll go.
(*He goes*.)
(*Off*) Ah yes, doctor.
(KATHERINE *paces up and down*. MARGARET *peeps to get a
glimpse of the doctor*.)

MICHAEL: I wonder how thorough they have to be, then?

MARGARET: He's black.

SUSAN: My God.

MARGARET: Oh yes, you'd be amazed – they're all black these
days.

SUSAN: I meant . . .

MARGARET: Oh, you don't know what it's like. Just what it's
come to . . .

DOUGLAS: Shut up, Margaret.
(KATHERINE *steadies herself*.)

MICHAEL: Are you all right, Mom?

KATHERINE: Not really.

MRS JACKSON: Why don't you sit down, dear? It's a shock, you
see. You can't help it. It comes as a terrible shock, even if
you're expecting it . . . and it's always worst when the
second one goes. You know; when both parents . . . oh yes,

there's going to be a gap. It's going to . . . oh yes . . . We're all going to miss her. I shall miss her. I don't know who we'll get in here now. It's going to be very odd and none of you are going to have no reason to come back here any more, are you? I don't know how we'll all go on, I'm sure. She and me, we were the last, the last of the old ones. We went through a lot. She was a good woman really, when my hubby . . .

KATHERINE: Mrs Jackson . . .

MRS JACKSON: Yes? Yes, dear?

KATHERINE: You don't have to stay, you know. You could go home if you wanted to.

MRS JACKSON: Oh.

KATHERINE: I mean, don't feel you have to stay.

MRS JACKSON: Oh well . . . if you don't need me . . .

KATHERINE: I'm sure we can manage. I mean, I don't mean to be rude . . .

MRS JACKSON: No, no . . . well, I can't do anything until the doctor's gone. I tell you what; maybe I'll slip home . . .

KATHERINE: Yes, yes.

MRS JACKSON: All right then.

(GEOFFREY *returns. They meet in the doorway.*)

Is it Dr Mucky-bee?

GEOFFREY: I don't know.

MRS JACKSON: It'll be night relief, I expect. Anyway, I'll pop back when he's gone . . .

GEOFFREY: Oh, thank you, Mrs Jackson, yes, do, do!

MRS JACKSON: Right.

(*She goes.*)

KATHERINE: Thank God for that. Should I . . . should I go in . . .?

GEOFFREY: No, no . . . sit down, just relax.

(*Silence.*)

MARGARET: I wonder if he's got any Codeine?

GEOFFREY: Oh dear, are you still . . .?

DOUGLAS: Go and ask him.

KATHERINE: What did he say?

GEOFFREY: Nothing, nothing. I told him she was under the doctor, it was all expected really. It wasn't a surprise.

MARGARET: I wouldn't say that, Geoffrey.

GEOFFREY: Oh no, no – it was a terrible shock, terrible . . .

MICHAEL: Terrible. I'll have to move. How long will I have to get out?

GEOFFREY: Out of where?

MICHAEL: I'll have to move now!

GEOFFREY: Oh, you'll be all right.

MARGARET: You'll have to buy somewhere. Don't go throwing your money away on rent.

DOUGLAS: But he's leaving the country.

GEOFFREY: What?

MICHAEL: Well, I'm, you know, I'm applying all over, I might . . .

GEOFFREY: He won't leave.

MICHAEL: How do you know?
     (GEOFFREY *smiles at him*.)
     Heh?

GEOFFREY: If you've got a job, be grateful!

MICHAEL: What a drag! I just wanted to get through this period of uncertainty.

DOUGLAS: Your life, you mean?

KATHERINE: What do you think he's doing now, then?

GEOFFREY: The doctor? Oh well, you know, he just has to, you know . . .

MICHAEL: Check she didn't swallow the pill bottle for a start-off! (KATHERINE *gets up*.)

GEOFFREY: Michael . . . (KATHERINE *sits down again*.)

MICHAEL: Well, where is it? I wouldn't put it past her. I've searched the house. And it was her birthday, maybe she thought, I'll get 'em while they're all here!

MARGARET: It wasn't pills, Michael. That wasn't what killed her.

KATHERINE: Please, please!

GEOFFREY: Yes, look, please, please; I'm sure the pill bottle will turn up and let's, hah ha . . . not go giving the chap ideas, heh? Walls have ears, you know, so . . . ha ha! That's all we need, ha ha! Let us leave cause of departure to the professionals, shall we? Ha ha . . . that's his job, that's what he's paid for and I'm sure . . .

KATHERINE: What have I done?

GEOFFREY: What?

KATHERINE: What have I done? I'm sorry, I'm sorry, everyone.

MARGARET: Why, what for?

KATHERINE: I'm sorry, Susan.

SUSAN: What for?

MARGARET: I don't see that you've got anything to be sorry for, Katherine, have you? It's not you . . .

KATHERINE: Mother would be alive now, should be alive now . . .

MARGARET: Oh yes,yes, she should! I know, exactly; this is what I said; it doesn't add up, it doesn't add up at all!

KATHERINE: No, no, no, it doesn't! You're right! I did it, all right?

GEOFFREY: Now, shh, sh, sh . . .

KATHERINE: No!

GEOFFREY: Dear, just let the doctor . . .

KATHERINE: Oh, shut up, Geoffrey! I did it, all right? OK? You're right – it doesn't add up, you're right, she could have gone on for years yet! She was picking up, wasn't she? But she didn't want to! She didn't want to, Margaret! She'd had enough, so . . . Oh God . . .

MARGARET: So . . . what?

KATHERINE: I helped her.

GEOFFREY: Shhh . . .

MICHAEL: Not with the pills?

MARGARET: No?

KATHERINE: Yes.

GEOFFREY: No, no, no . . . now wait a minute, just all hold on a moment. Let's not get, you know . . . The doctor's in there now and he'll, umm, I mean we don't know . . .

KATHERINE: We do, Geoffrey, we do! Stop pussy-footing around, all right? You saw what happened!

GEOFFREY: Me?

KATHERINE: Yes, for God's sake!

GEOFFREY: I saw nothing!

KATHERINE: Didn't you? Oh my God! Blind as well . . . I killed her . . . I . . .

GEOFFREY: No, no, no . . . I don't believe, not for an
    instant . . .
MARGARET: You did what, Katherine?
GEOFFREY: Please! Please . . . The doctor is in the next
    room . . . if we could choose our words . . .
    (*Silence.*)
SUSAN: Oh my God . . .
KATHERINE: I'm sorry, Susan.
SUSAN: (*Shakes her head.*) I should have stayed in Shepton
    Mallet.
KATHERINE: So I'll just . . . I'd better just . . .
GEOFFREY: No, no, wait. Everybody just hold tight . . .
KATHERINE: No, I'll . . .
GEOFFREY: Katherine, please! No one is going anywhere, not
    yet! Sit down. OK . . . OK . . . now look, OK . . . right, so
    let's not . . . let's keep calm . . . try to be a little bit clear
    before we go rushing off. Just tell me . . . tell me exactly
    what you think happened umm . . .
KATHERINE: I know what happened.
GEOFFREY: What you think you did.
KATHERINE: I know what I did.
MARGARET: What did you . . .?
KATHERINE: Sorry, Margaret.
MARGARET: Why? I mean, what did you do? What on earth
    could possess you?
GEOFFREY: All right Margaret, thank you, now please, please
    could I just, you know . . . I'd like to be absolutely clear
    about this – whatever Katherine did or didn't do and maybe
    she doesn't even know . . .
KATHERINE: I do! Every tiny detail!
GEOFFREY: OK, fair enough – you think you know, but let's not
    jump to any conclusions – that's the doctor's job . . . isn't it,
    Douglas?
    (GEOFFREY *is hoping for support,* DOUGLAS *says nothing.*)
    And if he should find anything untoward – and I must say,
    she looked perfectly normal to me, you know,
    considering . . .
MICHAEL: But she would, Dad!

46

GEOFFREY: Hold on, Michael, please! I want to be absolutely clear about this. This is important now, I mean when things like this happen, it's all too easy to read things into things – we all naturally feel all sorts of things; a loved one, you know . . . and we feel distressed, guilty perhaps, confused, is that it, Katherine?

KATHERINE: No.

GEOFFREY: A feeling that you could have, should have, done more?

KATHERINE: More?

GEOFFREY: A feeling of inadequacy, such that you now think . . .

KATHERINE: Oh yes, oh yes; she wouldn't die! First the pills, she couldn't swallow the bloody things!

MARGARET: Oh my God!

KATHERINE: Then the carrier bag – ridiculously too big.

MARGARET: What?

KATHERINE: Then the pillow . . . what have I done?

MARGARET: Katherine . . .

KATHERINE: She begged me! She begged me!

GEOFFREY: Shh . . . OK, OK . . . shh . . . right well, so she . . . right, well, the doctor's with her now. He's not come through yet, has he? So . . .

MICHAEL: So what, Dad?

KATHERINE: I'd better go and . . . I'll go and tell him.

GEOFFREY: You will go nowhere.

KATHERINE: I can't just sit here!

GEOFFREY: Yes you can.

KATHERINE: I can't bear it!

GEOFFREY: What?

KATHERINE: Waiting!

GEOFFREY: One step at a time. Now the pills, just tell me . . .

KATHERINE: What?

GEOFFREY: How did she . . . I mean, did she . . . did you give her the bottle?

MARGARET: Please, Geoffrey, I can't take this! I don't think I wish to . . I'm sorry, I'm sorry . . . Why, Katherine?

GEOFFREY: Please, Margaret! Let me . . . this is important.

47

'Why' is not important. 'How' could be very important and it is important Katherine is clear in her own mind, before the doctor, I mean, just in case the doctor . . . should . . . we need to be clear.

KATHERINE: I am clear.

GEOFFREY: Good, good . . . then would you tell me . . . please, just how . . . unfortunately the detail could be, it may be important . . .

KATHERINE: Oh yes, it is! God, Geoffrey, do you think I don't know? If it was the Sainsbury's bag that killed her . . .

GEOFFREY: Shh . . . OK, very good; keep it down!

KATHERINE: If it was the Sainsbury's bag that killed her then it's murder. Don't worry, I know all about it! If it was the pills then it's possibly only aiding and abetting. If it's unclear whether it's the pills, the bag or suffocation by pillow, then it may only be manslaughter, all right? Yes – the detail is very important – that's probably what he's deciding right now! (*Silence*.) All right?

MARGARET: (*Moans quietly*) My God . . . Lord God in heaven . . .

GEOFFREY: Right, well, that's helpful so . . .

MARGARET: Oh my God!

MICHAEL: You mean you planned it, Mom?

GEOFFREY: Now she didn't say that! Now please, Michael.

KATHERINE: I didn't plan it, no.

GEOFFREY: Right, you see? Good, good!

KATHERINE: Not really, plan.

GEOFFREY: Of course you didn't.

KATHERINE: But for years, Michael, she made me promise; 'Never have me put away, Katherine.' I did try to discuss it with you once, Geoffrey, do you remember?

GEOFFREY: With me? My God, no – I have no recollection . . .

KATHERINE: No, I'm sure you haven't. 'Don't let me suffer.' 'If ever I lose my faculties, Katherine, promise me . . .' I promised her, you see? And when she did become very confused, after that first fall – didn't know who anyone was, where she was, then I started to read . . . Read every book in the library, every article in the papers about, you know . . .

48

and I knew, that's how I knew – and I felt I knew like friends
the people who . . . People have been to court you know,
have been tried, have been to prison even, for doing only
what I've done tonight. Oh God! Do you think . . . I'm so
frightened.

(*She goes to* DOUGLAS.)

GEOFFREY: Shh . . .

MARGARET: Then why on earth, if you knew . . .

DOUGLAS: Don't worry. Listen, we're all with you.

MARGARET: We're what?

DOUGLAS: You're not alone.

MARGARET: Well . . . I mean, of course she's not alone, we're
all here . . . where we like it or not . . .

KATHERINE: It was such a terrible mess! So squalid! She gagged
and choked . . .

MARGARET: Katherine! I think you'd better not tell us any
more . . .

KATHERINE: It was all . . .

MARGARET: In fact I wish you hadn't told us anything at all. I
don't think you should be saying this. Do you know just
what . . .

KATHERINE: Yes, yes!

GEOFFREY: OK, please, so it was a mess. We do have to know
what umm . . . but hopefully, Margaret, Katherine, I mean
let us keep our fingers crossed. We may be lucky. She was a
very old woman after all, she was under the doctor . . .

MICHAEL: So?

GEOFFREY: Well, who knows?

MARGARET: He should be out by now, if everything was . . .

GEOFFREY: Maybe, maybe not.

MICHAEL: Don't there have to be two doctors?

MARGARET: Oh, my God!

DOUGLAS: Only for cremations.

MARGARET: Mother will be buried.

GEOFFREY: Right. He'll need to know that, won't he?

MARGARET: Along with Father. If they allow it, of course. If
they allow it after something like this.

DOUGLAS: Oh, shut up!

49

MARGARET: Don't tell me to shut up!

DOUGLAS: You're not helping.

MARGARET: Don't tell me to shut up, she was my mother! And when Uncle Sid took his own life they wouldn't let him . . .

DOUGLAS: Shut up!

SUSAN: Why? Why today?

KATHERINE: The day you came back?

SUSAN: Right.

MARGARET: Her birthday.

KATHERINE: It was nothing to do with you.

SUSAN: I find that difficult to believe.

GEOFFREY: I don't think she even knew it was you, actually.

KATHERINE: She did. Oh, she did.

SUSAN: Yes, and I think that's why . . .

KATHERINE: Yes, all right, yes, you could be right! Yes OK, yes it did upset her – you were back and you were seeing her in that state. If you looked her in the eye you could see, for heaven's sake, that she knew exactly what was going on – and what was happening to her and she'd had enough. She wanted to die. She wasn't afraid to die . . .

DOUGLAS: Of course she wasn't.

MARGARET: How do you know?

DOUGLAS: It's only us, that aren't ready for it.

KATHERINE: Right! It was her choice, honestly!

DOUGLAS: That's the way it should be.

KATHERINE: Thank you, Douglas! Oh, thank you! I'm not a bad person then, am I?

DOUGLAS: Don't be daft.

KATHERINE: It was her wish.

DOUGLAS: Right. Are you all right?

KATHERINE: No, no, I'm not all right! Not all right at all! Bloody woman! She wanted me to do it, then fought me to the last! Oh Mother, Mother, Mother . . .

GEOFFREY: So . . .

KATHERINE: What the hell's he doing, Geoffrey? I'll have to . . .

GEOFFREY: No, no, it does take time.

MARGARET: Not this long.

50

GEOFFREY: Oh, I'm sure it does.

MARGARET: I suppose the police will be here next then, will they?

GEOFFREY: No, no, no . . . let's not . . .

MARGARET: They were with Uncle Sid, like a shot! Before they even got him out of the oven!

KATHERINE: Please!

MARGARET: I can't believe it. When it comes to death I think this family's jinxed. I've always thought so. Look at Dad – only fifty-six and no warning . . .

GEOFFREY: Please, if we could . . . umm, you know . . . If I could just . . . I'd like to be absolutely concrete about this before umm . . . Is this what happened? She tried to take her pills – too many perhaps, more than she should. She couldn't swallow them, choked, spat pills all over the floor . . .

MARGARET: Is that what happened?

GEOFFREY: We don't know, Margaret, I'm trying . . .

MARGARET: What about the Sainsbury's bag, where did that . . .?

GEOFFREY: Yes, yes . . .

MARGARET: (*Crossing to the bags*) Is this the bag?

GEOFFREY: I'm trying to . . .

MARGARET: This is full of Tupperware.

GEOFFREY: Yes . . . is it? Fine . . . (*To* KATHERINE) While you were not looking she picked a bag up off the table, did she?

MARGARET: Is this all my Tupperware?

GEOFFREY: And when you looked up off the floor where you were picking up pills, she'd put the bag over her head . . .

MARGARET: But if the bag was full . . .

KATHERINE: It wasn't like that.

MARGARET: I know it wasn't – there's half a trifle in here for a start-off!

GEOFFREY: But could it have been like that?

MARGARET: Have you lifted this bag?

KATHERINE: For God's sake; it was the pillow, if you really want to know; the pillow! I did it, Geoffrey! I put it gently to her face . . . very gently . . .

51

GEOFFREY: To wipe her mouth?

KATHERINE: No!

GEOFFREY: But that could have been your . . .

MICHAEL: Dad!

GEOFFREY: Sorry?

MICHAEL: You're being ridiculous! We can't lie our way out of this!

GEOFFREY: I'm not lying. .

KATHERINE: Well, it didn't happen like that.

GEOFFREY: Then help me, please! I'm trying to avoid avoidable complications!

MICHAEL: Then help Mom tell the truth!

GEOFFREY: All right, yes, yes, I am!

MICHAEL: You're not! And if you don't we'll all be in it.

GEOFFREY: I'm trying to find what the truth is!

MICHAEL: Well, you were there, weren't you?

GEOFFREY: I was not.

MICHAEL: Mom said you were there.

KATHERINE: He came in, Michael.

MICHAEL: OK; so what did you see?

GEOFFREY: It's not what I saw, Michael – it's how one interprets what one saw, or didn't see.

MICHAEL: Or chose not to see.

GEOFFREY: As indeed it is all down to how one interprets what your mother did or didn't do . . .

MICHAEL: Oh God, he's off! This isn't a courtroom, Dad, and you're not a bloody lawyer!

GEOFFREY: Oh, just shut up, Michael!

MICHAEL: No, I bloody won't!

KATHERINE: Please!

MARGARET: Michael's right. He's right, I'm afraid. This is . . . this isn't just a burglary, Geoffrey. They'll ask questions about this. They'll want to know the truth, I mean I'd love to lie but . . . which is why, Katherine, I wish you'd not said, I mean if we cover up we could all be in for it. They'll question us all . . . Oh God, why, Katherine, I cannot believe! Even if we say we know nothing about it . . . Now you've told us . . .

DOUGLAS: Margaret!

MARGARET: What?

DOUGLAS: Just stop being so bloody self-righteous!

MARGARET: Me?

DOUGLAS: Do you want to know the truth, you and Michael?

MARGARET: I do, yes! Yes I do, I can't believe, I can't start to imagine!

DOUGLAS: Well, the truth is, for a start-off; we're all as guilty as Katherine here, so . . .

KATHERINE: No!

MARGARET: Guilty?

DOUGLAS: Oh yes, yes we are, Katherine, believe me! So your mother's dead, why? Because we stopped forcing her to be alive! So don't you dare, Margaret . . .

MARGARET: We stopped . . .? She's dead because Katherine . . .

DOUGLAS: It's nothing to do with Katherine! That's a mere technicality!

MICHAEL: Oh now, come on . . .

DOUGLAS: Sorry?

MICHAEL: Well, come on . . . I mean, I don't call . . .

DOUGLAS: Why didn't you send her to hospital weeks ago?

MICHAEL: Me?

DOUGLAS: How long has she been coughing blood?

GEOFFREY: We didn't want her mucked about, Douglas.

DOUGLAS: Quite right too!

(KATHERINE *paces, she is restless.*)

It's all right, Katherine. But if she'd been a few years younger, you wouldn't let her cough blood, or dribble her antibiotics down her front, or spit out her tablets. If I was coughing blood, would you say, 'I don't want him mucked about'?

KATHERINE: Please . . .

DOUGLAS: She was dying, Katherine. The pain was getting worse. All her infections were getting worse. We could have treated them, we have the technology, but no – we didn't want her mucked about – or kept alive any longer than was absolutely necessary – we were all letting her die! Now what is worse . . . Margaret, Michael, what is worse: to do nothing or to do something positive? What's the difference morally, come on, I can see no difference! There is no difference, except that the one takes guts and I think it's bloody disgusting that she had to do it on her own!

KATHERINE: Oh, I didn't want to! I wanted to call out!

DOUGLAS: Right!

KATHERINE: 'Help me, someone!'

DOUGLAS: And you knew you couldn't! Disgusting!
(*To* MARGARET) And you now sit there . . .

MARGARET: Why are you getting at me?

DOUGLAS: Because all you're really worried about is blame! First it was Susan . . .

SUSAN: Me?

DOUGLAS: 'She killed her.' 'She killed her!'

MARGARET: I only meant . . . For God's sake! Honestly Susan, I only . . . I never . . .

DOUGLAS: And now Katherine, 'Why, Katherine, why?' Well, I'm telling you, we're all as guilty as the other, in fact the only person who shouldn't be feeling guilty right now is Katherine!

KATHERINE: Oh, Douglas!

DOUGLAS: So come on, less of this pious bloody self-righteous, holier-than-thou bit – I mean who was it said the other day, 'I wish she'd die'?

MARGARET: What?

DOUGLAS: 'If only Mother would die.' You said it.

MARGARET: I have never!

DOUGLAS: When we had that letter from the bank?

MARGARET: Katherine, Geoffrey, I have never! How could you? Anyway, anyway, saying something is one thing . . .

DOUGLAS: And wishing it is exactly the same! So . . . 'Why' is important, Geoffrey, not bloody 'How'. My God . . .

GEOFFREY: I'm sure, I'm sure . . . OK . . .

MARGARET: I never said that, I didn't! Why does he say these things?

GEOFFREY: But practically that doctor could come in here any second now . . .

KATHERINE: And I'll tell him the truth.

GEOFFREY: You could do that . . .

KATHERINE: Right.

GEOFFREY: But personally I think there's a good case here for saying absolutely nothing.

MICHAEL: Oh my God!

GEOFFREY: And keeping our voices down, please!

MICHAEL: And when he asks?

GEOFFREY: We know nothing. OK? We all know nothing. That might seem odd . . .

MARGARET: But Geoffrey, that could make us accessories!

DOUGLAS: Ha!

GEOFFREY: Listen, she was a very old, weak, frail woman and who knows . . . what Katherine did or didn't do, and I reserve my judgement on that, it may have had nothing to do technically with the cause of her death, so all I'm asking everyone to do is cross only one bridge at a time. I'm not asking anyone to lie . . .

MICHAEL: You are! My God, Dad!
(*There's a knock on the door.*)

GEOFFREY: Ahh . . . OK, one second please . . . Coming! Just for once do as I say, Michael, OK? I know what I'm doing!

MICHAEL: So do I!

GEOFFREY: OK! (*He goes.*)

MICHAEL: I know exactly what you're doing! He's extraordinary! He always said to me, 'I can read you like a book, Michael' What he forgets is, we're the same bloody book! I can read him too! I know what he's trying to do . . . every conflict in his life, he plays ostrich . . .

KATHERINE: Please . . .

MICHAEL: It won't work, not this time!

MARGARET: What are they saying? Can anyone?

MICHAEL: What yarn is he spinning?

KATHERINE: (*Nervously waiting*) Come on, come on . . .
(*They all try to listen.*)

MARGARET: How you could say . . .

DOUGLAS: Shut up!

MARGARET: I loved my mother!

KATHERINE: So did I! Margaret, so did I!

55

MARGARET: Well, if you don't mind me saying so, I think that's a very funny way of showing it!

DOUGLAS: If you don't shut up, Margaret . . .

KATHERINE: Has anyone got a cigarette?

MICHAEL: You don't smoke.

KATHERINE: This seems a pretty good time to start. (*She talks now out of nerves.*) What happens if . . . does anyone know? The procedure? They take me away, I suppose. What are they saying? I just want you to know Susan, we did try other ways . . .

SUSAN: You what?

KATHERINE: I mean, not other ways – other ways to help her, I just want you to know we did try everything so if you think I'm a terrible person . . .

SUSAN: I don't.

MARGARET: Is Dick all right for milking in the morning?

DOUGLAS: Pardon?

MARGARET: We're not going to be there, are we?

DOUGLAS: We weren't anyway.

KATHERINE: Maybe I should have moved back here to look after her.

DOUGLAS: Don't be silly.

KATHERINE: People do. People do give up their lives to look after their parents, don't they? What's so special about my life that I couldn't?

DOUGLAS: You tried! You had her at your place.

KATHERINE: God, she hated it. She left excrement all round the living room on purpose, of course. Ripped up everything that ripped! Maybe I should have persevered.

DOUGLAS: You were killing each other.

KATHERINE: We were! We were! Yes, yes, we were! We drove each other, oh yes, I had a breakdown, you see, maybe they'll take that into account except I don't think anyone knows; I was just overtired, that's what Geoffrey called it; 'You're overtired. Send her to Margaret's.'

MARGARET: Oh. She wouldn't come! We'd have loved to have her . . .

KATHERINE: We could have done that; sent her against her will,

56

like a parcel of concern all round the country, yes, maybe we should . . .

DOUGLAS: No! It was no answer. You did everything you could. She didn't want to go from place to place, travelling was a nightmare to her.

KATHERINE: We're all so far apart, you see, Susan, these days. We're all so far apart. So spread out and far apart. What are they are saying? Oh, I don't think I want to hear. I just wanted you to know that, Susan. I just wanted you to know that we did try . . .

MARGARET: Oh, we did. We all tried. We're so isolated, you see, where we are . . . it's difficult . . .

DOUGLAS: All you've done now is what she wanted.

KATHERINE: I hope so, God I hope so. What's Geoffrey saying, do you think? I hope he's not trying to . . . Oh God, I didn't do it to get away with it! I didn't! You just do what you have to do, don't you?

MICHAEL: I think he's going.

KATHERINE: What?

MARGARET: He's what?

(*They listen. The front door shuts.* MARGARET *goes to look.*)
Maybe he's just . . .
(GEOFFREY *comes back in.*)
Geoffrey, where's he . . .?

KATHERINE: He's not gone?

GEOFFREY: Well . . .

MICHAEL: Come on . . . what's happening, Dad?

GEOFFREY: Well, I have here a piece of paper . . .

KATHERINE: Has he gone?

GEOFFREY: The doctor has gone.

MARGARET: And is he coming back?

GEOFFREY: No.

KATHERINE: No?

MARGARET: You mean that's it?

GEOFFREY: Absolutely. That, Margaret, would appear to be it.
(KATHERINE *collapses into a chair and sobs into a cushion.*)
Katherine . . . Katherine . . . it's all right . . . Everything is hunky-dory – he's gone!

(*They all wait and watch.* KATHERINE *sobs and sobs.*)
Katherine . . . Katherine . . .
(*He tries to comfort her. She runs out and can be heard crying in the hall.*)
Oh dear . . . it's been a long day, you see. We were up very early.

MICHAEL: But the doctor.

GEOFFREY: What, Michael?

MICHAEL: I can't believe that's it, can you?

GEOFFREY: I told you . . .

MICHAEL: Told me what?

DOUGLAS: What did he say?

GEOFFREY: Nothing really. A few details – what to do with this . . . (*The piece of paper.*)

MICHAEL: And cause of death?

GEOFFREY: I didn't ask.

MICHAEL: You didn't ask?

GEOFFREY: In the circumstances, I thought . . .

MARGARET: He could be on his way to the police, of course.

GEOFFREY: No, no, no . . . I mean, I don't think . . . I mean, there was no hint that he was anything but satisfied.

MICHAEL: I don't believe it. Mind you, knowing the medical profession . . .

DOUGLAS: Do you?

MICHAEL: What?

DOUGLAS: You don't, so shut up.

GEOFFREY: I did say not to jump to conclusions.

MICHAEL: But for God's sake; she told us step by step!

MARGARET: She did, Geoffrey!

GEOFFREY: Margaret, listen to her – just listen! She's distraught! I know Katherine, deep down she's a very emotional person . . .

SUSAN: So what do you really think?

GEOFFREY: I think it was all a very nasty little mix-up. I think your mother was probably being very silly with her pills, Katherine tries to intervene, there's panic, pandemonium, pills everywhere, Mother has a seizure, or a stroke or something, Katherine is in shock, overcome with guilt – she

always felt guilty about Mother and there you have it!
(*The sobbing continues.*)

DOUGLAS: Shall I?

SUSAN: I'll go . . .

(SUSAN *goes out to comfort* KATHERINE.)

MICHAEL: So you think that's it?

GEOFFREY: I have a form here . . .

MICHAEL: So? So?

GEOFFREY: Well . . . What more do you want, Michael?

MICHAEL: I want the bloody truth, which is a damn sight more
than you do! She was my grandmother! I was looking after
her! Until tonight, I mean, when you can't even go to the
pub without coming home and finding someone's murdered
your grandmother.

GEOFFREY: Please!

MICHAEL: And you think you can just troll off home! What's the
bloody world coming to, heh? Wake up, Dad!

GEOFFREY: Now come on . . .

MICHAEL: That was no little mix-up! That was a deliberate act
and you know it!

GEOFFREY: She's confused! It's all part of her confusion,
coming to terms with . . .

MICHAEL: Your confusion, you mean! Your deliberate bloody
confusion! Why do you do it, Dad? Every issue, he does it all
the time; talks his way into the totally balanced, extremely
reasonable, see all points of view inertia! That's what you are
– a bloody inert gas!

GEOFFREY: Oh, thank you.

MICHAEL: Well, it's not bloody good enough! Not in this case!
And this won't just go away either! Not this! That doctor will
be back, mark my words. She can't get away with this! She's
my mother but she had no right!

DOUGLAS: She had every right!

MICHAEL: What?

DOUGLAS: She had every right.

MICHAEL: To break the law?

DOUGLAS: Oh, come on! Whose law? A mother makes a pact
with her daughter . . .

MICHAEL: The law of the blooming land!

DOUGLAS: OK, since when have compassion, courage and bloody guts been against the law of the land?

MICHAEL: Killing someone, bloody murder, is against the law!

DOUGLAS: Murder? Come on, Michael . . .

GEOFFREY: Now listen, please . . .

MICHAEL: She broke the law . . .

DOUGLAS: And if the law's wrong? It's only made by the likes of you and me and it's always years behind the times.

MICHAEL: Oh, don't be . . . My God, I'm not talking about traffic laws, about some trivial little transgression of regulations! Bloody hell, that's what he's trying to do, to trivialize!

DOUGLAS: Well, what are you talking about Michael; the fact that someone's actually finally made you feel something? That you're upset?

MICHAEL: Thou shalt not kill!

DOUGLAS: Oh God!

GEOFFREY: All right, Michael, thank you! Yes, we all know the Commandments!

MICHAEL: I don't think he does!

DOUGLAS: Oh, I do, I do; 'Thou shalt not kill' – except in war or by Act of Parliament, or . . .

MICHAEL: You know what I mean!

GEOFFREY: All right, well, not now, Michael, please.

MICHAEL: I'm not having him . . . I mean what's going on? Five minutes ago he was suggesting we were all guilty!

DOUGLAS: Too right! Except your mother maybe.

MICHAEL: I was looking after her!

DOUGLAS: Bravo! And a pretty terrible job you must have been doing, she was in agony!

MARGARET: Please!

DOUGLAS: What?

MARGARET: I still have my migraine, you know.

DOUGLAS: Well, go to bed.

MARGARET: Don't be silly. I think he's gone for a second opinion.

DOUGLAS: He should have asked Michael!

MARGARET: I'm going to look for a painkiller. He'll be back I
   think.
   (*She goes out to the kitchen.*)
DOUGLAS: He probably will.
GEOFFREY: No . . .
DOUGLAS: I didn't realize . . . it flushes them out, doesn't it,
   heh? I thought, I hoped we had at least got beyond the
   worshipping of ancient gods. But no; you're religious, then?
MICHAEL: When life suddenly starts becoming cheap . . .
DOUGLAS: Cheap? On the contrary!
GEOFFREY: I think we should be careful what we say here,
   Michael . . .
MICHAEL: When life is suddenly subject to the whims and
   momentary aberrations of people like my mother!
DOUGLAS: 'Momentary'? She'd thought about it for years.
MICHAEL: Worse! Worse! And when he . . . (*Geoffrey*) When
   he, a so-called Christian, can dilute everything he feels or
   maybe even once believed in, to a meaningless blather – a
   cover-up for a quiet life, I think we do need, yes, we do need
   something, you know . . . and when even the bloody doctor,
   if he really has gone, then by God, are we going mad? Then
   yes, I do think we need something a bit absolute, don't you?
   If we prove ourselves incapable of you know . . . then yes; I
   think we need to establish a few certainties!
DOUGLAS: He is religious! So what's the old book got to say on
   mercy-killing then? I don't recall anything either way.
MICHAEL: You mean you've read it?
GEOFFREY: Now, Michael, come on . . . a little hush . . .
MICHAEL: No, I won't bloody hush! Why did she do it? Why
   should I? I was, me and Mrs Jackson, we were . . . I used to
   get up every night, three times sometimes, we were looking
   after her . . .
DOUGLAS: And she begged your mother to help her end it all.
MICHAEL: Yes, yes and she begged me! She said lots of things!
DOUGLAS: And you ignored them? Is that what a person
   deserves at the end of a long life? Is that the price of living to
   old age? Didn't she deserve something better than that?
   'Ignore her she's rambling!' Great!

GEOFFREY: Very tricky . . . Oh shh . . .

> (KATHERINE *comes in with* SUSAN. *They cross towards the kitchen.*)
>
> Ahh, ahh, Katherine . . . feeling a bit better?

KATHERINE: I'm going to have a wash.

GEOFFREY: Oh good, that's the idea, yes, you'll feel better then.

SUSAN: Come on. Do we still have to boil a kettle?

KATHERINE: Cold water will do.

> (*They go.*)

GEOFFREY: (*Looking at his watch*) Then we'll have to make a few decisions, I suppose.

DOUGLAS: Just tell me one thing, Mike, one thing; what will you do when you get to that age, heh? Will you really be content to leave it all in God's hands? Have you thought about it? There's more and more people getting their telegrams now, you know. Forty years of retirement you could have now.

GEOFFREY: Oh my God!

DOUGLAS: Twenty years maybe of senility.

GEOFFREY: Oh Lor'!

DOUGLAS: Ten years of double incontinence.

MICHAEL: Don't be ridiculous! Not necessarily!

DOUGLAS: Not necessarily, no. It's a lottery, of course. I didn't know you were a gambler – have you looked at the odds? Studied the form? Have you by any chance been to the homes of the losers? I have, Michael – I watched both my parents rot in homes full of decaying hulks, tried to talk to my mother only to be drowned out by the sound of the woman sitting next to her pissing on the plastic chair. Watched my father being kissed by another man who thought he'd just found his wife. I could go on. Will you really leave yourself happily in God's hands as you shit in the corridor on your way to communal lunch? Or will you beg someone to help you? Hoping to God they're not Christian! Beg someone to give you that final bit of dignity, to help you to a decent peaceful death . . .

GEOFFREY: It's difficult, isn't it?

DOUGLAS: I'll tell you what you'll do – you'll do what we're all doing – you'll leave it till it's too bloody late! Until your brain's gone or you've had a stroke and nobody understands your begging grunts!

MICHAEL: Listen! (*Bangs his beer glass on the table; it breaks, glass and beer going everywhere.*) Oh hell!

DOUGLAS: Whoops!

GEOFFREY: Now you see! Oh Michael . . .

MARGARET: (*Coming in, alarmed*) What on earth . . .

MICHAEL: Bollocks!

(*He throws a chair across the room out of his way so that he can get at the broken glass.*)

MARGARET: Michael!

KATHERINE: (*Coming in*) What's happening?

(SUSAN *comes in.*)

GEOFFREY: Nothing, nothing! Now, Michael . . .

MICHAEL: Oh shit!

(*He pushes past them into the kitchen.*)

DOUGLAS: It's always the ones you'd least expect . . .

SUSAN: What's the matter?

DOUGLAS: I do believe he's really upset.

KATHERINE: Oh dear, shall I speak to him?

DOUGLAS: I thought he was incapable . . .

GEOFFREY: Maybe if we just leave him, Katherine . . .

(*She is going.*)

KATHERINE: I'm just putting the towel back.

GEOFFREY: Ah OK, OK . . . I'd better . . . (*He follows her out.*)

DOUGLAS: Well, well, well . . . A good night so far . . .

SUSAN: I should never have come back.

DOUGLAS: (*Clearing up the broken glass*) Oh, why not? Murder, mystery, suspense, Dream Topping on your trifle; what more could you want?

SUSAN: It's a madhouse.

DOUGLAS: Well, now they're doing away with the larger asylums, you know – integrating us into the community . . .

SUSAN: Is it always like this?

DOUGLAS: In what way, pray? If it was always like tonight, there'd be none of us left, would there?

MARGARET: My God, you're sick!

DOUGLAS: Terminal dear, terminal, and you?

SUSAN: Do you think the doctor spotted it? If there was anything to spot?

DOUGLAS: I'm sure.

MARGARET: He'll be back then, won't he? I knew it!

DOUGLAS: Why? Why should he? It's routine to him.

MARGARET: For God's sake, Douglas!

DOUGLAS: What?

MARGARET: It didn't sound routine to me!

DOUGLAS: No, but you're not a doctor. He's on the front line. He sees what he sees, makes decisions, hundreds a week, day and night, round the clock . . .

SUSAN: Plays God, you mean?

DOUGLAS: Ugh! If you must use such . . . I suppose, yes, he does, if that's what we force him to do. Rather him than an ancient dictat.

(MICHAEL *comes in with a bandaged hand and a dustpan and brush.*)

Ah Michael! Talking of ancients . . .

MICHAEL: Oh shit, you've done it.

SUSAN: You're bleeding . . .

MICHAEL: I know, I know.

(*He goes back out.*)

DOUGLAS: (*Calls*) Doctor! Doctor!

MARGARET: I wish you wouldn't wind him up, Douglas!

DOUGLAS: Ah . . . that's what it is!

MARGARET: What?

DOUGLAS: He's clockwork, of course! In the age of the microchip!

MARGARET: You can't take it, can you?

DOUGLAS: What?

MARGARET: You know what I mean.

DOUGLAS: I'm sure I don't.

(KATHERINE *comes back in.*)

Katherine . . . are you all right?

(GEOFFREY *follows her in.*)

KATHERINE: I don't know, am I?

GEOFFREY: Of course you are.

64

KATHERINE: I think I've crossed over into another world tonight, Douglas. I don't think I will ever be the same again.

GEOFFREY: You will.

KATHERINE: I don't want to be, thank you very much!

GEOFFREY: Oh right, right, I see . . .

(*Her vehemence silences them all.*)

KATHERINE: No sirens yet, then?

GEOFFREY: No . . .

KATHERINE: Please God, don't let them lock me up!

GEOFFREY: They won't, they won't!

KATHERINE: No? So what do you think the doctor . . .? I don't understand.

MARGARET: Neither do I.

DOUGLAS: I do.

MARGARET: You would. That's typical.

GEOFFREY: I think he was happy, Margaret.

MARGARET: I don't care if he was delirious! He should be ashamed of himself!

KATHERINE: Margaret . . .

MARGARET: I'm not being personal, now, Katherine, I'm not judging what you did, whatever I might think of that, now, I'm just saying . . .

KATHERINE: Thank God for useless doctors!

DOUGLAS: Or ones that secretly understand.

KATHERINE: Why secretly?

DOUGLAS: That's the way it is.

KATHERINE: Why? I hate that more than anything! Oh . . . now I'm getting angry. Why, why, why?

(*They sit in silence.* GEOFFREY *looks at his watch.*)

GEOFFREY: Well . . .

MARGARET: Poor Mom.

DOUGLAS: Poor Katherine.

GEOFFREY: Well . . . Time moves on . . . What do we all feel, ummm, is the next move?

MARGARET: We'll have to let people know, won't we?

KATHERINE: What? Who?

MARGARET: Family, Katherine!

KATHERINE: Oh . . . oh yes . . . not tonight.

MARGARET: No, but in the morning . . .

KATHERINE: Yes . . .

GEOFFREY: I was thinking more immediately – the procedure . . .

MARGARET: Like what, Geoffrey?

GEOFFREY: Well, in our case there's dogs to be walked. That's number one, I think . . .

KATHERINE: I'm not going home.

GEOFFREY: Ah . . .

KATHERINE: So do what you like.

GEOFFREY: Right, well, I'd better, umm . . . I see . . . I'll have to maybe pop home, walk Candy then come back perhaps, possibly.

KATHERINE: Do whatever you like, Geoffrey.

MARGARET: And what do we do if anyone else comes?

GEOFFREY: I really don't think . . .

MARGARET: Like the police . . .

(*The front door slams.*)

You see!

GEOFFREY: Mrs Jackson. Surely that will just be . . .

KATHERINE: Get her out!

GEOFFREY: Out? But I did say . . .

KATHERINE: Out!

(MRS JACKSON *knocks and enters.* GEOFFREY *blocks her way.*)

GEOFFREY: Mrs Jackson . . . could I just . . . How nice of you to . . . could we . . .

(*He ushers her back out.*)

MRS JACKSON: Oh . . . everything all right?

GEOFFREY: Oh yes!

(*They go.*)

MARGARET: I think I shall have to . . .

DOUGLAS: Just go to bed!

MARGARET: Oh, no, no . . . but I shall have to find a darkened room. It's the eyes, you see, with migraine.

DOUGLAS: Go and lie down.

MARGARET: If anyone else does come . . .

DOUGLAS: Oh, we'll let you know. You won't miss out, don't

worry. We'll tell them you want to be arrested as well!

KATHERINE: Please!

DOUGLAS: Sorry! (*To* SUSAN) Bad taste. I'm the one that always laughs at funerals. Sorry, Katherine.

MARGARET: I'll just . . .

(*She goes out, bumping into* GEOFFREY *as she does so.*)

GEOFFREY: Sorry . . . sorry, Margaret! Katherine . . . Mrs Jackson was just suggesting . . .

KATHERINE: Tell her to sod off, Geoffrey.

GEOFFREY: Ahh . . .

KATHERINE: Go and walk the dogs together, anything!

GEOFFREY: Ah . . . OK . . . OK, I'll, umm . . . yes, it's nothing vital, I'll . . .

(*He goes.*)

KATHERINE: Sorry about that. What am I doing? Oh dear . . . He's really got on my nerves tonight. Poor Geoffrey. I think underneath he's terrified. That makes two of us . . . he must have seen . . .

SUSAN: So it was, as you said, a deliberate . . .

KATHERINE: Yes! My God; yes, yes, yes! Why does nobody . . .

SUSAN: Sorry, I've been away, remember.

KATHERINE: Why on earth did you come back?

SUSAN: We all make mistakes.

KATHERINE: Oh don't, don't! Have I? That's what I want to know. Tell me, someone, please!

DOUGLAS: I've told you.

KATHERINE: Yes, you understand, don't you, Douglas? You see, Susan, it wasn't just that she was in pain, though that was terrible to watch, but more than that, you came back and she couldn't even tell you to get out! Or tell you how much she loved you, or . . . when you can no longer express what you feel, because of the pain or whatever, then my God . . . it doesn't you see, mean that you don't still feel it deep down. I know she was feeling, oh, feeling so much and to express that, to be able to talk about what you feel, that's as much a part of being alive as having legs that work, isn't it?

DOUGLAS: Absolutely.

67

KATHERINE: And when that's gone, that ability to express, should we not have the right, one final right . . .

DOUGLAS: To a decent death.

KATHERINE: That's it – and that right must be hers, mustn't it? Oh God, mustn't it? (*Takes a deep breath, sighs and shakes her head.*) That we should come to this, Susan.

SUSAN: I have a feeling that wherever she is, she's laughing at us now.

KATHERINE: Yes, yes! Ha . . . it's all right for some! It's all right saying, 'Help me Katherine!' Bloody woman! What about Katherine? I wish I'd left home when you did, I tell you .

SUSAN: If I'd really left home I wouldn't be here now, would I? I tried maybe . . .

KATHERINE: You made a blooming good job of it if you ask me! Twenty-five years! How could you do it? Did you forget us? Did you never want . . . Did you know the pain . . .? (SUSAN *starts to sob.* KATHERINE *is stopped in her tracks.*)

SUSAN: Don't be horrible to me, please! Why is everyone so awful? Why did you never come looking for me?

KATHERINE: (*Comforting her*) Don't, don't . . . Oh what a mess! We thought you'd come back. We could never believe you'd really gone. When you left we never . . .

SUSAN: When I was thrown out!

KATHERINE: No!

SUSAN: 'Never darken my door again.' That's what she said.

KATHERINE: You were pregnant.

SUSAN: Right! That's just the sort of help a young girl needs, isn't it?

KATHERINE: You weren't married.

SUSAN: Exactly!

KATHERINE: She didn't mean it.

SUSAN: Oh she did, she did!

DOUGLAS: Does it matter now? You were all so bloody proud it wasn't true. That's the truth of it.

KATHERINE: Is that what it was?

DOUGLAS: It's best forgotten, isn't it?

KATHERINE: Of course it is. Of course it is! Just so long as you're happy.

68

SUSAN: Oh yes.

KATHERINE: Good.

SUSAN: My second marriage has just broken up.

KATHERINE: Oh . . .

SUSAN: My kids stubbornly refuse to grow up. My fault – I always told them not to. Forbade them to have any ambition, or soil their hands in the temple of Mammon, so . . .

DOUGLAS: They're not working?

SUSAN: God, no!

KATHERINE: What are their names?

SUSAN: Cloud . . .

KATHERINE: Sorry?

SUSAN: That's right. And Rain. At least you've saved me the trouble of trying to explain that one to Mom, thank you. Don't get me wrong – they're wonderful children . . . sorry, people – it just never occurred to me that it might one day be difficult for them, so . . . we're all at square one, them and me. Very exciting, all learning together, which is one reason why, I suppose, I'm back. But I certainly didn't . . . little did I . . . ohh . . .

(KATHERINE *and* SUSAN *embrace and cry, letting go at last.* DOUGLAS *eventually reads the paper.* GEOFFREY *looks in, sees what's happening and goes out again.*)

KATHERINE: Don't ever go away again, little sister! Promise me! Promise me . . .

(SUSAN *smiles at her.*)

DOUGLAS: What are your plans?

SUSAN: Mine?

DOUGLAS: Yes.

SUSAN: Would that I had some.

DOUGLAS: Well, I shall be going back to the farm in the morning. If we're not all arrested, that is!

SUSAN: Farmer Douglas! I can't imagine . . .

DOUGLAS: I'm not a farmer.

KATHERINE: You are.

DOUGLAS: You're born a farmer, but that's another story. Margaret will doubtless stay here for a bit, search the loft and chair linings for hidden fortunes.

KATHERINE: She's wasting her time.

DOUGLAS: Don't spoil her little pleasures. If you have no plans, why don't you come back with me?

SUSAN: Back with you?

DOUGLAS: If you fancy it.

SUSAN: Ha . . .

(*They look at each other.*)

Can I sleep on it?

DOUGLAS: I'm off at first light.

SUSAN: I don't think that would be any answer, do you?

(*They remain staring at each other.* MICHAEL *comes in, a tea towel round his hand. It is held high in the air.*)

MICHAEL: The point is, Douglas . . .

DOUGLAS: Are you still up?

MICHAEL: The point is . . .

KATHERINE: What have you done to your hand?

MICHAEL: (*Holding it up in the air to stop the bleeding*) It's a really deep cut.

KATHERINE: Does it need stitches? The hospital . . .

MICHAEL: Ha! They'd probably amputate – if they thought it more cost effective, or quicker . . . The point is, Douglas, do we adapt what we believe to the way we live our lives, or should we adapt the way we live our lives to what we believe?

DOUGLAS: Ah . . . that's what you've been cooking in the kitchen, I see!

MICHAEL: Well?

DOUGLAS: Well . . . what did you say?

MICHAEL: Should we adapt what we believe to the way we live our lives or should we adapt the way we live our lives to what we believe?

DOUGLAS: Well . . . I'm afraid you've got me there, Ayatollah, can I sleep on it?

MICHAEL: If you can sleep! I think you should.

(*He sits down.*)

KATHERINE: Your hand.

MICHAEL: *Remembering to hold it up*) My hand is fine.

(*Silence.*)

So . . . what are we waiting for now then?

DOUGLAS: You can go to bed if you want to.

MICHAEL: Go to bed? Do you really think . . . ?

(GEOFFREY *looks in.*)

GEOFFREY: All right? How are we all, um . . . What I've decided to do, just to let you know. Mrs Jackson has kindly agreed to, or insisted rather . . . ahh . . .

(MRS JACKSON *passes through to the kitchen.*)

MRS JACKSON: All right? If I could just get the bowl and towel, I won't get in your way. I'll put a clean nightie on her though, dear, everything else can wait till morning, can't it? (*Picks up the rubbish basket.*) Oh, look at me . . . that's habit that is! Every night I'd empty this, remove all matches and you know; anything that might burn or spill. Oh, she was a terror.

GEOFFREY: Very good, very good.

MRS JACKSON: We never knew what we'd find in the morning, did we, Michael? She was supposed to be bedridden but if she put her mind to something . . . Anyway . . . (*Going out*) It's going to take a bit of getting used to.

GEOFFREY: Well, then . . .

MICHAEL: You can get used to anything, can't you?

GEOFFREY: What's that?

(*He doesn't answer.*)

Well . . . everything seems to be quiet now. That seems to be it for tonight by the looks of things. There's nothing else we can do, is there? So, I'll get off now, walk Candy and come straight back, all right? If you're all right, Katherine . . . If you're going to get some sleep now . . .

MICHAEL: You're going all the way home and coming back?

GEOFFREY: Life goes on, Michael.

(MARGARET *comes back in.*)

MARGARET: What's happening?

DOUGLAS: Nothing.

MARGARET: I thought I heard the door.

DOUGLAS: No one else is coming, Margaret, not tonight.

MARGARET: I was sure I heard . . .

DOUGLAS: What do you want – your pound of flesh?

(*She is stung, there is an embarrassed silence.*)

71

MARGARET: (*To* GEOFFREY) It's the farm, you know.

GEOFFREY: What's that?

MARGARET: That's what it is, people don't realize, they just think; oh there's another successful farmer! They don't realize! What are we supposed to grow? There's too much of everything. They say, milk – we put our money into milk. They say there's too much milk. We think, pigs! Then find there's swine fever in the next valley! Well, it's not my fault, Douglas, so don't take it out on me! Aghh . . .
(*Her head hurts, she sits down.*)

GEOFFREY: I think there are enough beds if anyone is ready to, er . . . I've checked the front bedroom. Mrs Jackson says she'll help with bedding. If we could all get a little sleep, we're obviously all getting a little fractious, it's been quite a day.
(*No one moves.*)
It did occur to me, just by the by, before we all go our separate ways, we must arrange Christmas.

KATHERINE: What?

DOUGLAS: Shouldn't we arrange the funeral first?

GEOFFREY: Good point, good point!

KATHERINE: Shouldn't you go if you're going?

GEOFFREY: I suppose I must unfortunately, if we don't want problems all over the kitchen floor . . . I'll be as quick as I can . . .

KATHERINE: Just go, Geoffrey.

GEOFFREY: I'm going, I'm going . . .
(MRS JACKSON *comes in with a bowl of hot water and a towel.*)
Ah, all right, Mrs Jackson?

MRS JACKSON: I won't be long.
(*They watch her go through.*)

GEOFFREY: Right then. And just in case . . . if anyone else should come, I'm sure they won't but if the door was to go, are we a little clearer now . . .?

KATHERINE: Perfectly! There is no confusion, Geoffrey! It's all perfectly clear, thank you very much. Now go! Just go!
(*He can't; that was not the answer he wanted. Eventually he sits down.* KATHERINE *grasps* SUSAN's *hand and holds it tight.*)

Afterword

This should not be regarded as an 'issue' play about euthanasia. All I've attempted to do is bring a group of people together who find themselves increasingly out of their depth. The play is a look at the quality of their lives, my contention being that 'being alive' – 'life' is very much a relative experience. If we don't face up to its end, if we insulate ourselves from death, we diminish our own existence. In this way the characters in the play are stunted by their attitudes. Their inability to confront the issue is a handicap as disabling as the blindness or deafness that they from time to time affect. When Katherine having done the deed says, 'I've crossed over into another world tonight . . .' That's exactly what it feels like to her – a breaking through, a profound transition that will affect and inform every moment of her future life.

The play is deliberately not about professionals. That is why no one on stage has real medical or legal knowledge, and this leads to the most important point. At no time after the death do the characters *intentionally* argue or debate the issues involved. Such discussion as does arise – between Douglas and Michael in particular – happens only when characters find themselves pushed to the point when they can no longer keep silent. They are not entirely stupid or insensitive – they are aware of what's happened, of the feelings of other people in the house, of the fact that there is a dead body in the next room. The time of night itself informs the atmosphere. Douglas would rather say nothing, while Michael is simply making a desperate attempt to rationalize the extraordinary events of the night. It is only in this context and in the knowledge that they may, at any moment, be called upon to answer for what has occurred, that they find themselves arguing.

STEPHEN BILL